Haunted Britain

50 Ghost Stories Based on True Paranormal Encounters Across England, Scotland and Wales

Hourglass History

Copyright © 2023 Twisted Tales. All rights reserved.

No part of this publication may be reproduced, stored in a retrieval system, or transmitted in any form or by any means, electronic, mechanical, photocopying, recording, or otherwise, without written permission of the publisher.

Table of Contents

Introduction 1
Chapter 1: The Tower of London Ghosts....................... 4
Chapter 2: Borley Rectory in Essex.............................. 9
Chapter 3: The Brown Lady of Raynham Hall............ 13
Chapter 4: The Pendle Hill Witches............................ 17
Chapter 5: The Roman Soldiers of York...................... 21
Chapter 6: The Hampton Court Ghosts 25
Chapter 7: Pluckley, Kent - Echoes of the Past 29
Chapter 8: The Ancient Ram Inn, Wotton-under-Edge - Whispers of the Old... 33
Chapter 9: The Princes in the Tower............................ 37
Chapter 10: Lady Lovibond 42
Chapter 11: The Screaming Spectres of Fyvie Castle.. 45
Chapter 12: The Glastonbury Abbey Monks 48
Chapter 13: The Ghostly Piper of Duntrune Castle 52
Chapter 14: The Ghostly Soldiers of Edgehill............. 56
Chapter 15: The Restless Souls of the Mary Rose....... 61
Chapter 16: The Ghosts of Naseby Battlefield 65
Chapter 17: The Cursed Skull of Bettiscombe Manor. 69
Chapter 18: The White Lady of Avenham Park, Preston 74
Chapter 19: The Drowned Souls of Canewdon Church 78
Chapter 20: The Haunting of the SS Great Britain 83
Chapter 21: The Haunting of the Golden Fleece, York 87

Chapter 22: The Ghost of Anne Bronte at Scarborough 91

Chapter 23: The Phantom Highwayman of Dartmoor . 95

Chapter 24: The Ghost of Greyfriars Bobby, Edinburgh 99

Chapter 25: Dorothy Southworth of Samlesbury Hall, Lancashire 103

Chapter 26: The Mackenzie Poltergeist, Greyfriars Kirkyard, Edinburgh 107

Chapter 27: The Ghosts of Kenilworth Castle, Warwickshire 111

Chapter 28: The Chillingham Castle Ghosts, Northumberland 115

Chapter 29: The Ghosts of Bodmin Moor, Cornwall . 119

Chapter 30: The Ghosts of Warwick Castle, Warwickshire 123

Chapter 31: The Ghosts of the Theatre Royal, Drury Lane, London 127

Chapter 32: The Ghost of Lady Howard, Dartmoor .. 131

Chapter 33: The Ghosts of the Banqueting House, London 135

Chapter 34: The Ghost of the Lady in Green, Thetford Priory, Norfolk 139

Chapter 35: The Ghost of Sker House 144

Chapter 36: The Ghost of Richard III in Leicester..... 148

Chapter 37: The Haunting of the Jamaica Inn, Cornwall 152

Chapter 38: The Grey Lady of Glamis Castle, Scotland 157

Chapter 39: The Ghost of the Green Lady, Stirling Castle, Scotland 161

Chapter 40: The Phantom Drummer of Edinburgh Castle, Scotland 165

Chapter 41: The Headless Phantom of Hever Castle, Kent 169

Chapter 42: The Spectres of Avebury Stone Circles, Wiltshire 174

Chapter 43: The Ghosts of Athelhampton House, Dorset 178

Chapter 44: The Spirit of Margaret Pomeroy, Berry Pomeroy Castle, Devon 182

Chapter 45: The Screaming Woods of Dering, Kent . 186

Chapter 46: The Highgate Vampire, Highgate Cemetery, London 190

Chapter 47: The Green Children of Woolpit 195

Chapter 48: The Gwyllgi, the Dog of Darkness in Wales 199

Chapter 49: The Black Lady of Bradley Woods, Lincolnshire 203

Chapter 50: The Blue Lady of Temple Newsam, Leeds 208

Beyond the Pages: Your Part in the Story 212

Introduction

The rain beat down on the cobblestones, playing a melancholic rhythm as if the earth itself was weeping. If you listened closely, amid the chorus of the drizzling rain and the soft whispers of the wind, you could hear the echoes of a past long gone but not forgotten. Britain, with its sprawling moors, ancient castles, and narrow alleyways, has always been a land steeped in mystery and magic. It's a place where the line between reality and the supernatural seems precariously thin. Every town, every village, and every road holds a story. Some speak of heroism, some of romance, but the ones that linger, that haunt our dreams and unsettle our nights, are tales of the unknown - of ghostly apparitions, restless souls, and unexplainable phenomena.

Ghosts are not just stories or remnants of a superstitious past; they are Britain's silent witnesses. They traverse its lands, from the rugged Highlands of Scotland to the historic depths of London, from the windswept coasts of Wales to the serene English countryside. Their tales are woven into the very fabric of the nation. And like the best tales, they've evolved, becoming a mix of history, hearsay, and a generous dash of imagination. A kind of whispered folklore, passed from one generation to the next, growing, morphing, and becoming legends.

This book is a testament to these spectral tales. Within these pages, you will find 50 ghost stories, each rooted in a real location, anchored by genuine historical events. But, like all legends, they do not remain static. Over time, they transform, adapting to the era, the storyteller, and the listener. As you delve into these tales, be forewarned: while they are grounded in Britain's storied past, they have been liberally laced with the fiction of the present. These are not strict historical accounts but rather a blend of fact and fiction, designed to chill the spine and make the reader reconsider every creak in the night.

Why this blend of history and imagination, you might wonder? Because sometimes, to understand the essence of a ghost story, to genuinely feel the chill it intends to deliver, we must venture beyond the mere facts. Truth, after all, can be stranger than fiction, but fiction can amplify the truth, make it palpable, and give it life – or in this case, afterlife.

Britain's landscapes are enchanting, with their lush green pastures, rugged cliffs, and ancient landmarks. But beneath the beauty lies a darker world, one filled with sorrow, love, revenge, and mystery. Each ghost, spirit, or entity represents a piece of that mosaic, a fragment of Britain's rich and often tumultuous history. From royalty betrayed to innocents wronged, from soldiers who never left their battlefields to lovers forever in search of reconciliation – their stories are myriad.

As you embark on this journey, expect to be transported to places where time seems to stand still, and the past bleeds into the present. Picture the Tower of London on a foggy night, the echoes of history reverberating through its stone walls, telling tales of betrayal and ambition.

Visualize the quiet village of Pluckley, where the line between the living and the dead seems almost non-existent. Or the vast moors of Cornwall, where legends and reality become indistinguishable.

It's worth noting, however, that these stories, though enriched with fiction, hold an element of truth. They have been witnessed, felt, and experienced by countless individuals. They've been the subject of investigations, both sceptical and believing. They've been the spark for debates, discussions, and, often, fear. And they've become a part of the British identity, a testament to a history so rich that it refuses to stay buried.

In this collection, the intention is not just to scare, but to fascinate, to intrigue, and to introduce you to a Britain you thought you knew. A Britain where every corner has a story, every shadow a secret. It invites you to step into the mist, to listen, to see, and to believe – even if just for a moment – in the world that exists just beyond our grasp.

So, dear reader, as you turn the page, remember: history never truly dies in Britain. It lingers, whispers, and sometimes, if you're truly attuned, it reaches out to touch you. Dive into these tales with an open mind and let the spirits of Haunted Britain guide you through the mists of time.

Let the journey begin.

CHAPTER 1:

The Tower of London Ghosts

Harold stepped off the last rung of the tour bus and stretched his legs. He had always been fascinated by history, particularly England's bloody and tumultuous past. And what better place to begin his exploration than the Tower of London, a cornerstone of English history?

The air was crisp, biting into his lungs with each breath. The massive stone walls of the Tower loomed above him, casting heavy shadows in the midday sun. Harold could sense the weight of centuries hanging over the fortress.

He had opted for the audio-guided tour. He wanted to walk the Tower at his own pace, letting his imagination run wild. As he made his way through the various sections, he was particularly drawn to the stories of those who had met tragic ends within its walls. Anne Boleyn, Henry VIII's second wife, executed for treason, and the young Lady Jane Grey, queen for just nine days before she was overthrown and later beheaded. Both tales were heartbreaking, full of political intrigue and personal betrayals.

But as the afternoon wore on, the crowds began to thin. Harold found himself wandering more secluded parts of the Tower. A narrow corridor led him to a small chapel, its entrance dimly lit. Curiosity piqued, Harold decided to step inside.

It was silent save for the occasional gust of wind that crept through the ancient windows. Rows of old wooden pews stretched ahead, and at the front stood a humble altar.

Harold was about to turn and leave when he heard it—a soft, mournful humming, its melody echoing faintly through the stone walls. He froze. It sounded close, like it was coming from within the chapel. Straining his ears, he tried to pinpoint the source.

Slowly, almost imperceptibly, the humming transformed into a delicate voice, singing a sorrowful lullaby. Harold's heart pounded as he followed the sound, which drew him to a pew halfway down the aisle.

And there she was.

A translucent figure, clothed in an ornate, old-fashioned dress, her head bowed as she sang. Her pale skin seemed to glow, casting a soft, ethereal light around her. Mesmerized, Harold took a step closer, and as he did, the woman slowly raised her head.

Their eyes met, and Harold felt a jolt of recognition. Those haunting, sorrow-filled eyes were unmistakably Anne Boleyn's, as depicted in many portraits he had seen. But there was no malice in her gaze, only profound sadness.

Almost instinctively, Harold lowered his head, a gesture of respect. When he looked up again, the figure was gone. The chapel was once again silent and empty.

Shaken, Harold quickly exited and found himself back in the corridor. Trying to shake off the eerie encounter, he decided to continue exploring. The path led him downwards, spiralling staircases bringing him to the bowels of the Tower.

As he descended further, the atmosphere grew colder, more oppressive. He could feel the weight of the Tower's history pressing down on him. Every step echoed loudly, a stark reminder of his solitude.

Suddenly, from the darkness ahead, another sound joined his echoing footsteps—a soft sobbing. Harold hesitated for a moment, then decided to push on. The weeping grew louder, more distinct, guiding him to a dimly lit cell.

Peering inside, Harold was met with another apparition. This one was younger, with golden hair cascading down her back. She sat on the cold, stone floor, her head buried in her hands as she wept.

Despite her ethereal appearance, Harold could feel the depth of her anguish, almost as if it reached out from the past, piercing the veil of time. The realization struck him; this was Lady Jane Grey.

Before he could react, a door banged somewhere in the distance, breaking the spell. Harold spun around, searching for the source. But the sound wasn't repeated. When he looked back into the cell, Lady Jane was gone.

Heart racing, Harold decided he had experienced enough for one day. He needed to get out, to breathe fresh air and shake off the heavy gloom that had settled over him. As he retraced his steps, a chilling breeze whispered past him, carrying with it faint, mournful whispers, snippets of long-forgotten conversations.

Emerging into the daylight, Harold took a deep breath, feeling an immediate sense of relief. But as he made his way towards the Tower's exit, he couldn't shake off the feeling that he was being watched.

He turned around one last time, and for a brief moment, he could have sworn he saw two figures standing side by side, gazing down at him from one of the Tower's high windows. But when he blinked, they were gone.

That night, back in his hotel room, Harold tried to dismiss his experiences as products of an overactive imagination. Yet, as the hours ticked by, an unsettling silence enveloped his room. It was broken only by the faint ticking of the room's vintage clock.

Sometime past midnight, Harold was roused from a restless slumber by a cold wind sweeping across his face. Disoriented, he sat up. The room's curtains billowed inward, despite the windows being firmly shut. Confused and anxious, he reached for the bedside lamp. Its weak light revealed an unsettling sight: the hotel room's door was ajar.

Suddenly, a mournful lullaby echoed through the room, its notes chilling him to the bone. The same tune he had heard in the Tower chapel. He watched in horror as shadowy figures materialized, their translucence making them nearly indistinguishable from the dark.

The figure with haunting eyes approached, her fingers reaching out. "Stay with us," she whispered, her voice a blend of desperation and sadness. The room grew colder, and Harold felt an overpowering pressure, as if invisible hands were pushing him down into the bed.

And then, with a deafening silence, it all stopped. The figures vanished. The lullaby faded. Only the tick-tock of the room's clock remained. Harold was alone, but the weight of the room's darkness felt almost tangible.

The following morning, hotel staff found Harold's room locked from the inside. It took them nearly an hour to break it down. Inside, they found the room undisturbed, save for the vintage clock which had stopped at precisely 3:33 am. But of Harold, there was no trace.

CHAPTER 2:

Borley Rectory in Essex

Dark clouds hung ominously over Borley Rectory as Nathaniel Westwood approached the large, imposing house. It stood isolated, surrounded by dead trees that seemed to stretch their gnarled branches towards the heavens, as if begging for salvation.

The rectory was a place of dark legends, a hotspot of paranormal activity that had frightened the townsfolk for generations. But Nathaniel, a professor of paranormal studies at Cambridge, had heard it all before. There wasn't a haunted house in England he hadn't visited, a ghost he hadn't debunked. He believed Borley Rectory would be no different.

"Probably rats in the walls or drafts causing doors to close," he thought to himself.

The rectory stood still, eerily quiet, as if it were watching him. Despite his scepticism, a shiver ran down Nathaniel's spine.

Once inside, the air was stale, like a tomb, causing him to cough. The echoes of his footsteps on the creaky floorboards felt intrusive. Portraits of former residents stared down from the walls, their eyes shadowed and hollow.

Nathaniel set up his equipment in the main hall: cameras, voice recorders, electromagnetic field detectors. He wanted to capture any anomaly, any proof of the afterlife. As night began to fall, a quiet murmur ran through the house. A soft whispering, growing louder and more distinct, until it sounded like a cacophony of mournful voices.

His voice recorder picked up the chilling voices, voices that begged for release, voices that screamed in pain. Yet, when he played back the recording, there was only silence.

As he explored the house, the atmosphere grew oppressive. Shadows flitted across walls, even though there was no one there to cast them. Cold spots appeared and disappeared mysteriously. At one point, he distinctly felt a hand brush against his, the touch icy cold. When he looked down, he saw the faint outline of a woman in a flowing white dress.

In the library, Nathaniel found a journal dated back to the 1800s, chronicling the experiences of a priest who had lived there. The journal spoke of strange occurrences: Objects moving on their own, walls that bled, ghostly apparitions. The priest wrote of trying to perform an exorcism, but he seemed to have gone mad in the process, the final pages filled with frantic scribbles and the repeated words, "They won't leave. They won't leave."

Nathaniel, ever the sceptic, continued his investigation. The dining room's grand chandelier swung of its own accord. The old piano in the corner played a haunting tune even though no one was near it. Suddenly, a force seemed to push him from behind, sending him sprawling on the floor.

As he tried to get up, he felt hands grasping at him, pulling him back down. Panicking, he managed to free himself, running into the hallway, but the doors slammed shut, trapping him inside. The air grew thick, making it hard to breathe. From the darkness emerged figures, translucent and ethereal, their eyes devoid of light.

Nathaniel felt an overwhelming sense of despair. These were souls, trapped for eternity, tormented and in pain. And they were angry. The very walls of the rectory seemed to pulsate with their anguish.

Trying to find an escape, he stumbled upon a sealed room. As he broke the lock and entered, a rush of cold air hit him. Inside was an altar, covered in dust and cobwebs, but at its centre lay a fresh, still-beating heart. The room seemed to be the epicentre of the haunting, the source of the evil that plagued Borley Rectory.

The spirits grew more aggressive. They surrounded Nathaniel, their hands reaching out, their faces twisted in anger and pain. Despite his fear, he knew he had to do something. Searching frantically, he found a vial of holy water in his bag, which he threw on the altar. A blinding light filled the room, and a deafening scream echoed throughout the house.

When the light faded, Nathaniel found himself alone in the rectory. The oppressive atmosphere was gone, replaced by an eerie silence. However, the relief he felt was short-lived.

As he made his way to the front door, it opened on its own, revealing the dark expanse outside. But instead of the path that led to the village, there was only an abyss, an endless void of darkness.

From the abyss, hundreds of hands emerged, reaching out for him, pulling him in. Nathaniel screamed, but no sound came out. The last thing he saw before everything went dark was the rectory, standing tall and imposing, its windows glowing with an otherworldly light.

Back in the village, the townsfolk spoke in hushed tones about the man who had dared to venture into Borley Rectory and never returned. The house stood as a testament to the unknown, a place where the living and the dead intertwined, and where some, like Nathaniel Westwood, lost themselves forever in its dark embrace.

CHAPTER 3:

The Brown Lady of Raynham Hall

Drenched in shadows, Raynham Hall stood tall amidst the barren landscapes of Norfolk. Its gothic spires, jutting from the main structure, seemed like fingers reaching for the cloudy skies. For those who dared approach its heavy wooden doors, a profound sense of dread enveloped them, for they were entering the domain of the infamous Brown Lady.

Jacob Tremaine, a photographer with a penchant for the unknown, had come to Raynham Hall not for its striking architecture or its manicured gardens, but to capture the elusive spectre that roamed its halls. Legends whispered she was Lady Dorothy Walpole, betrayed and imprisoned within the walls of the grand mansion. The many who claimed to have seen her spoke of her brown brocade dress, her pale face, and her empty eyes, forever trapped in sadness.

With his old box camera set up in the main hall, Jacob waited. The night outside was dark, with only the occasional crack of lightning illuminating the rooms. As the hours slipped by, an oppressive silence settled, broken only by the occasional drip of water or the soft scuttle of unseen rats.

Then, as midnight approached, Jacob heard it - the soft rustling of fabric moving down the corridor. He strained his ears, and it grew louder, accompanied now by soft, forlorn sobs that echoed mournfully throughout the house. Jacob readied his camera.

As he looked through the viewfinder, the temperature in the room plummeted. Every instinct screamed at him to flee, but he remained rooted to the spot, mesmerized by what he was witnessing.

Emerging from the shadows, the figure of a woman came into focus. Her dress, though faded, was clearly of a bygone era, and it flowed around her as if submerged in water. Her face, however, was what held Jacob's attention. It was as pale as moonlight, and her eyes – they were hollow, pits of eternal despair.

Jacob's finger hesitated over the camera's shutter. The Brown Lady's gaze met his, and in that instant, a rush of emotions flooded him: sorrow, anger, and an overwhelming feeling of being trapped. But overriding all was her sadness, a soul-crushing weight that threatened to pull him under.

Gathering every ounce of courage, Jacob pressed the shutter, capturing the apparition on film. The flash briefly illuminated the entire hall, and in its aftermath, the figure was gone, leaving Jacob alone with the chilling silence.

He left Raynham Hall as dawn began to break, the haunting image of the Brown Lady etched into his memory. The photograph he took that night would become one of the most famous ghost photographs in history. Yet, while the world marvelled at its clarity and debated its authenticity, Jacob was tormented by the spirit's emotions, her sadness clinging to him like a shroud.

Weeks turned to months, and Jacob became a recluse, avoiding his friends and family, his once bright studio now darkened and abandoned. The weight of the Brown Lady's sorrow was an ever-present companion, suffocating him, drawing him deeper into despair. Sleep, when it came, was filled with nightmares – visions of being imprisoned, of walls closing in, and of an eternity of loneliness.

One evening, a close friend, Clara, concerned by Jacob's rapid decline, visited him. She found him seated in his darkened studio, the photograph of the Brown Lady placed prominently on his desk. Picking it up, Clara felt a chill run through her, but she also recognized the deep despair in the spectre's eyes.

Clara, a woman with a deep connection to the spiritual world, realized what needed to be done. The spirit of Lady Dorothy Walpole had imprinted her emotions onto Jacob through the photograph, chaining him to her eternal sorrow. To free him, they would need to return to Raynham Hall and confront the Brown Lady once more.

The following night, with the photograph in hand, Clara and Jacob stood once again in the grand hall of Raynham Hall. As midnight approached, the familiar rustling echoed through the corridors, growing louder until the ethereal figure emerged from the shadows.

Clara stepped forward, her voice unwavering. "Lady Dorothy, we understand your pain, your despair. But you cannot bind another to your sorrow. You must let him go."

The Brown Lady's hollow gaze shifted from Jacob to Clara, the air around them growing colder. The weight of her despair pressed down on them, threatening to suffocate them. Yet Clara held her ground, holding up the photograph and began to recite a chant, calling upon the spirits of the land to free both Lady Dorothy and Jacob from their chains of sorrow.

The ground trembled, and a blinding light enveloped the room. When it subsided, the Brown Lady was gone, and in her place stood a door. Clara, sensing its significance, approached it. Behind it lay Lady Dorothy's true prison, the room she had been confined to during her life. Opening the door, Clara released the trapped energy, setting the spirit of Lady Dorothy free.

As dawn broke, Jacob felt the weight lift off him. The crushing despair was gone, replaced by a sense of peace. Clara, exhausted, leaned on him for support. They had confronted the haunting sorrow of Raynham Hall and emerged victorious.

Yet, as they left, a soft whisper echoed through the corridors, a reminder that the Brown Lady, though freed from her prison, would forever roam the halls of Raynham, a testament to love betrayed and a life lost too soon.

And in the deep shadows of the mansion, one could still hear the soft rustling of a brown brocade dress.

CHAPTER 4:

The Pendle Hill Witches

In the shadow of Pendle Hill, Lancashire, lay a village that seemed untouched by time. Its thatched-roof cottages, narrow winding streets, and the ever-present silhouette of the hill looming over it made for a picturesque, yet unsettling sight. The village was known for its dark past, a past that was whispered about in hushed tones, especially when the fog rolled in.

In 1612, the village was rocked by accusations of witchcraft. Twelve individuals were accused, tried, and ten were executed, hanged for their supposed crimes. The village seemed to sigh in relief, believing the dark times were over. But as the years went by, strange occurrences began. Livestock found dead, crops failing, and children waking up screaming from nightmares that felt too real.

Emma, a journalist, had always been fascinated by the supernatural. The tale of the Pendle witches was too alluring to resist. She had heard about the village's haunted reputation, about the shadowy figures seen wandering the hill on moonless nights, and about the eerie chants that sometimes echoed in the wind.

Arriving in the village, Emma felt the weight of hundreds of eyes upon her, though the streets were nearly empty. Checking into the village inn, she was met with curt nods and suspicious glances. She knew she was an outsider, and the village was protective of its secrets.

The inn was an old establishment, wooden beams and stone floors that had seen centuries pass. Emma was given a room at the very end of the corridor. The wooden floors creaked underfoot, and the dim light from the lanterns cast eerie shadows.

That night, as the wind howled outside and rain pelted against the windows, Emma was awakened by a soft chanting. Curiosity piqued, she followed the sound, leading her out into the stormy night, towards Pendle Hill.

The ground was muddy, her feet sinking with every step. The chanting grew louder, a mournful, rhythmic cadence that seemed to beckon her. At the summit, she found herself amidst a circle of stones. The remnants of a ritual, long forgotten, yet hauntingly familiar.

Suddenly, the chanting stopped, replaced by a cold, deafening silence. The fog around her thickened, and the full moon revealed the silhouettes of ten women, standing around her, their gazes empty, their faces pale and gaunt.

Emma froze, realizing she stood in the midst of the very witches who were executed all those centuries ago. Their voices rose once more, not in a chant now, but in an accusatory tone. "Why have you come here?" one of them hissed. "Are you here to condemn us further?"

Panicking, Emma tried to retreat, but her feet wouldn't obey. The circle tightened around her, their skeletal fingers reaching out. Each touch was like a burn, searing her skin, drawing her energy.

"I only wanted to know the truth," Emma managed to choke out, tears streaming down her face.

One of the witches, who seemed to be their leader, stepped forward, her hollow eyes boring into Emma's. "The truth? The truth is that we were betrayed. Betrayed by those we called neighbours, friends. They took our lives, but our spirits were bound to this land, forever to wander and seek retribution."

"We have waited," another witch whispered, her voice filled with malice. "Waited for someone like you, curious enough to seek us out."

Emma's heart raced, realizing the gravity of her situation. The witches were not just spectres of the past; they were vengeful spirits, searching for a vessel to continue their dark work. And she had walked right into their trap.

Using every ounce of her strength, Emma began to recite a prayer, hoping it might offer some protection. The witches hissed and recoiled, but they did not retreat. Their grip on her tightened, their intent clear.

Yet, as Emma's voice grew louder, a brilliant light began to emanate from her, pushing the spirits back. The leader, resisting the most, screamed in rage, "You may have escaped, but others will come. And we will be waiting!"

The light became blinding, and when it subsided, Emma found herself alone on Pendle Hill, the ghosts of the witches nowhere in sight.

Exhausted and traumatized, Emma fled the village at dawn. The innkeeper, seeing her dishevelled state, only nodded, a mix of sympathy and warning in his eyes.

Back in her city apartment, Emma tried to put the horrifying events behind her. She decided not to publish her experiences, fearing they'd either not be believed or would attract more unsuspecting souls to Pendle Hill.

However, the past was not done with her. Each night, as she drifted to sleep, she'd hear the faintest echo of chanting, a chilling reminder that the witches of Pendle Hill were waiting, hungry for the next curious soul to venture into their domain.

And sometimes, in the dead of night, she would wake up, feeling the cold touch of skeletal fingers on her skin, and the whisper of the leader in her ear: "We will always be waiting…"

CHAPTER 5:

The Roman Soldiers of York

York was a city of heritage, its cobbled streets and ancient buildings bearing witness to the weight of history. Among the many historical sites, the Treasurer's House stood out. With its timeless charm and grandeur, the house was both a popular tourist spot and a subject of whispered legends among the locals.

In 1953, a young plumber named Graham was summoned to the Treasurer's House to work on its antiquated heating system. The job required him to descend into the cold, damp basement. With a flashlight in hand, he stepped down, the ambient sounds of the world above fading away.

The basement was vast, its stone walls echoing with the memories of time. As Graham navigated the sprawling underground labyrinth, he stumbled upon a portion where the floor was inexplicably lower, almost as if it had been a road.

As he shone his light, Graham caught a peculiar sight: the top half of a Roman soldier walking on the old road, his lower half concealed by the current floor level. The phantom continued its march, oblivious to Graham's presence. Moments later, a series of similarly garbed soldiers followed the first, all marching in disciplined formation, their faces etched with determination and weariness.

Frozen in place, Graham's mind raced. Had he breathed in some toxic fumes? Were his eyes deceiving him? Yet, the ghostly parade continued, each soldier appearing more real and tangible than the last. Their armour clanked softly, and the dim torchlight of ancient times reflected off their shields.

At the rear of this spectral march was a senior officer on a horse, giving orders in Latin. Graham's heart raced as he recognized the insignia and attire, realizing he was witnessing a legion that had been lost to time.

As the last soldier disappeared into the wall, Graham, drenched in sweat, scrambled out of the basement. He shared his harrowing experience with the caretaker of the Treasurer's House, expecting disbelief. Instead, the old man nodded, his face pale.

"You've seen them too," he murmured.

The old man told Graham of the house's dark history, of the Roman road that once ran through where the basement now lay, and of the many sightings of the ghostly legion over the years. They were believed to be the spirits of Roman soldiers who died defending the city, their souls forever bound to the path they once guarded.

The caretaker also shared whispered rumours of those who had tried to interact with the phantoms. Those few unfortunate souls were found lifeless in the basement, their faces twisted in horror, their bodies bearing no mark but their souls seemingly sucked out of them.

Graham left the Treasurer's House, vowing never to return. He tried to put the encounter behind him, but the memories persisted, invading his dreams and turning them into nightmares. Night after night, he found himself on that old Roman road, surrounded by the ghostly soldiers, their hollow eyes staring accusingly at him, their hands reaching out to drag him into their eternal march.

One evening, unable to bear the weight of the haunting visions, Graham decided to face his fears. He returned to the Treasurer's House, descending once more into the abyss of the basement. Lighting a candle, he waited.

It didn't take long. The familiar clinking of armour reached his ears, and the torch-lit phantoms began their march. But this time, Graham stepped onto the old road, standing in their path.

The first soldier approached, his eyes void of emotion. As he drew closer, Graham could feel the cold, a numbing void threatening to consume him. Gathering his courage, he reached out to touch the apparition.

The world twisted around him. Suddenly, Graham found himself amidst a fierce battle. Roman soldiers clashed with barbaric invaders, the cries of the dying filling the air. An enemy warrior lunged at Graham, who narrowly evaded a fatal blow. As he stumbled and fell, the ground gave way beneath him, sending him plummeting into darkness.

When Graham opened his eyes, he was back in the basement. The Roman soldiers were gone, but the weight of their presence lingered. A chilling realization dawned upon him. He hadn't merely seen a glimpse of the past; he had lived it, even if just for a moment.

Weeks turned into months, and Graham's life became a torturous cycle of haunting visions and sleepless nights. He became a recluse, shunning the outside world, consumed by the phantoms of the Roman soldiers. His health deteriorated, and an insidious cold took root in his bones.

One fateful night, driven by madness and desperation, Graham returned to the Treasurer's House for the last time. He descended into the basement, murmuring a prayer, ready to join the legion in their eternal march.

His lifeless body was discovered the next day, lying on the old Roman road. The look of sheer terror on his face told a tale more horrifying than words ever could. The city of York continued its timeless march, and the Treasurer's House stood silent, guarding its dark secrets, waiting for the next soul curious enough to peer into its depths.

CHAPTER 6:

The Hampton Court Ghosts

Hampton Court Palace, with its sprawling courtyards, intricate tapestries, and long hallways, was both a monument to the glories of the past and a relic bearing a thousand untold secrets. Among the myriad of tales woven into the very fabric of its walls was the chilling legend of Catherine Howard, one of the unfortunate wives of Henry VIII.

Emma, a historian in her late twenties, had recently joined the staff at Hampton Court. Passionate about Tudor history, she was living a dream. Days turned to nights as she delved deeper into the annals, researching every nook and cranny, every whispered secret.

One evening, as the sun dipped below the horizon and the palace was bathed in a golden hue, Emma found herself alone in the library. A breeze rustled the curtains, and an odd chill permeated the room. Lost in her work, she suddenly heard the faint strains of a melancholy song.

Following the sound, she wandered through the hallways, the song growing louder. It seemed to emanate from the Haunted Gallery, the very place where Catherine Howard had made her final, desperate plea to the King. As Emma approached, she caught a glimpse of a spectral figure: a young woman, her face etched with despair, her mouth agape in a silent scream. The spectre raced down the corridor, her feet barely touching the ground, her eyes wide with terror. As quickly as she appeared, she vanished, leaving behind an overwhelming sense of anguish.

Emma's heart raced. She had read about Catherine's apparition, how she'd been dragged back to her rooms through this very hallway, her cries echoing in the stone corridors. But reading about it and witnessing it were worlds apart. She needed to know more.

Over the next few weeks, Emma's obsession grew. Every night, she'd find herself at the Haunted Gallery, waiting. One evening, as midnight approached, the air grew cold, the kind of cold that sinks into the bones. The mournful song began once again. But this time, as Catherine's apparition appeared, she wasn't alone. Behind her, shadowy figures, their faces obscured, reached out for her, their fingers gnarled and grotesque.

Emma, her breath fogging in the freezing air, felt an icy hand grasp her arm. She turned to see another ghostly figure, a man, his eyes hollow, his face twisted in rage and jealousy – King Henry VIII himself. His gaze fixed on Emma, and the world around her blurred.

She found herself in a different era. The sounds of revelry echoed through the palace. Dancers swirled in bright garments, their laughter light and carefree. Among them, she saw Catherine, young and vibrant, her laughter infectious. But as the night wore on, the atmosphere shifted. Whispers spread like wildfire. Catherine was summoned, and Emma followed.

The trial was swift and brutal. Accusations of betrayal, documents, testimonies – the weight of it all crushed the young queen. And then, that desperate sprint down the gallery, trying in vain to reach the king, to plead her innocence. Emma felt Catherine's despair, her heartbreak. As the axe fell, the world plunged into darkness.

Emma awoke with a start. The Haunted Gallery was empty, the early morning sun casting elongated shadows. Her head throbbed, the weight of the emotions she'd experienced still fresh.

Days turned into nights, but Emma could no longer differentiate them. The palace's corridors echoed with whispers, the walls closing in. Every shadow seemed to hide a ghost, every sound a harbinger of doom. The boundary between the past and present began to blur.

One evening, as a storm raged outside, Emma once again found herself in the Haunted Gallery. The candle in her hand cast flickering shadows, the darkness around her almost palpable. As the clock struck midnight, the melancholy song began its haunting refrain.

From the shadows, Catherine emerged, her gaze fixed on Emma. But she wasn't alone. Surrounding her were countless other spectres, their faces contorted in pain and anger. And there, towering above them all, was King Henry VIII, his presence oppressive, his wrath palpable.

Emma tried to move, to scream, but her body refused to obey. The ghosts advanced, their voices melding into a cacophony of anger, regret, and sorrow. The King, his face inches from hers, whispered words that chilled her to the bone, his breath cold and fetid.

As the sun rose, the staff found Emma in the Haunted Gallery, her body cold, her face twisted in horror. The echoes of the past had claimed another soul, the boundaries between life and death forever blurred.

The Hampton Court Palace stood silent, its secrets buried deep within, waiting for the next curious soul to tread its haunted hallways.

CHAPTER 7:

Pluckley, Kent - Echoes of the Past

Pluckley is a picturesque village, its rolling hills, and cobblestone streets seemingly frozen in time. But it had another, darker reputation: it was said to be the most haunted village in England.

Liam, a journalist in his mid-thirties with a penchant for the paranormal, had travelled to Pluckley after hearing rumours about its haunted history. Armed with a notebook and a healthy scepticism, he planned to spend a week investigating the supernatural claims, hoping to debunk some myths and perhaps find a story or two worth telling.

His first night was uneventful. He walked through the village, admiring its charm, and found a small inn for lodging. The innkeeper, a wiry old man named George, had deep-set eyes that hinted at many sleepless nights.

"That village's seen more than its fair share of sorrow," George murmured as Liam signed the guestbook. "If you're here for the ghosts, lad, be careful what you wish for."

Liam chuckled, dismissing George's warning as the ramblings of an old man.

The next day, Liam set out to explore. His first stop was the old blacksmith's shop. Legend had it that a blacksmith once fell in love with a noblewoman. Their love was forbidden, and in his despair, the blacksmith hung himself. Passersby claimed to have heard the clanging of metal and seen an apparition of a man in ragged clothes.

As Liam approached, a cold breeze sent shivers down his spine. The air grew heavy, thick with sorrow. He heard the faint sound of metal striking metal, echoing in the distance. A shadow darted past the window. It looked human, yet distorted, as if viewed through rippling water. Then, as quickly as it appeared, it was gone.

Shaken, Liam quickly noted down his experiences and moved on.

That evening, as the sun dipped below the horizon, Liam ventured to the village's hanging tree, where the notorious highwayman Robert DuBois was said to have met his end. Whispers among the villagers spoke of a shadowy figure seen hanging from the tree, swinging gently in the wind.

Liam approached the tree cautiously. Its gnarled branches stretched out like skeletal fingers, and the leaves rustled even though there was no wind. As he stared, a silhouette began to form. It was the figure of a man, suspended in mid-air, his face a mask of terror. The figure's eyes locked onto Liam's, filled with an eternal anguish, before it faded away, leaving nothing but the whispering leaves.

Liam's scepticism had all but evaporated. He felt a growing dread, a sense that the village was alive, watching him. That night, he found it difficult to sleep. The walls of the inn seemed to pulse with a life of their own, and distant screams echoed in his ears.

The following days were a blur of encounters. At the old mill, he heard the soft laments of a young woman, said to have been a mill worker who died tragically. At the village's crossroads, he saw ghostly apparitions of men and women, walking aimlessly, their faces contorted in pain.

But the most chilling experience was yet to come. On his last night, Liam decided to visit the old church graveyard. It was said to be the resting place of the Red Lady, a noblewoman who roamed the grounds, searching for her lost child.

As Liam walked among the tombstones, a dense fog enveloped the area. He could barely see a few feet in front of him. The air grew cold, and a deep silence settled, broken only by the faint cries of a baby.

Liam's flashlight flickered, its beam catching a glimpse of a woman in a red dress. Her face was obscured by a veil, but her eyes – those eyes were filled with a raw, primal agony. She floated towards Liam, her hand outstretched, her fingers inches from his face.

"Help me find him," she whispered, her voice a hollow echo. The world around Liam began to spin, the fog thickening, the cries growing louder. He felt an icy grip around his heart, squeezing, tightening.

When the villagers found Liam the next morning, he was lying in the graveyard, his eyes wide open, a look of sheer terror etched on his face. He was alive but unresponsive, trapped in a world between the living and the dead.

Pluckley, with its dark secrets and restless spirits, had claimed another victim. The echoes of the past continued to reverberate through its streets, waiting for the next unsuspecting soul to cross its path.

CHAPTER 8:

The Ancient Ram Inn, Wotton-under-Edge - Whispers of the Old

The village of Wotton-under-Edge was as peaceful as any other in England, but at its heart lay the Ancient Ram Inn. A building that defied time, with stone walls that seemed to have absorbed centuries of pain, joy, love, and most notably, terror.

Daniel, a photographer with an interest in the paranormal, had been drawn to the Inn ever since he'd seen a photo of it in a dusty old magazine. There was something about the building that called to him. It wasn't its beautiful, archaic architecture or its historic significance. It was something deeper, darker. The Inn had stories to tell, and he wanted to capture them through his lens.

He checked in, met by the innkeeper, Mrs. Emilia Gray, an old woman with eyes that held the weight of the world. Her hands were calloused, her back slightly bent, but her gaze was sharp.

"Not many come here willingly," she remarked with a raspy chuckle.

Daniel, ever the sceptic, brushed it off with a smile, "It's just for some photographs, ma'am."

Nightfall came quickly, the evening sun replaced by a darkness that seemed thicker than usual. With his camera in hand, Daniel decided to explore the inn. The wooden floors creaked under his weight, and the walls seemed to close in on him as he navigated the narrow hallways.

In the old Bishop's Room, he set up his camera. There were stories of this room being the most haunted. A bishop had reportedly been murdered here, and many claimed to see his spirit wandering, endlessly trapped.

As Daniel looked through the viewfinder, he felt a chill. Adjusting his focus, he noticed a figure, a silhouette of a man in ecclesiastical robes, staring directly at him. He blinked, and it was gone.

His heart raced, but he convinced himself it was just his imagination. Yet, he couldn't shake off the feeling of being watched. The room's temperature seemed to drop by several degrees. A voice, faint but unmistakable, whispered in his ear, "Leave this place..."

Panicking, he grabbed his camera and rushed out of the room, the voice echoing in his head.

He found himself in the attic, which had been turned into a small museum showcasing artifacts from the inn's past. The most unsettling was a collection of children's shoes, said to have belonged to children who had disappeared over the years. As he observed them, he felt a tug at his shirt. Turning around, there was nothing. But then, he heard soft giggles and saw shadows darting around the corners of the room.

The walls seemed to pulse, and the room filled with murmurs of the past. Whispers of children, their innocent laughter now a haunting melody. One voice stood out, "Help me... please..."

He stumbled downstairs, desperate to get out, but the inn had other plans.

He entered what used to be the pagan burial ground before the inn was built. Stories spoke of rituals and sacrifices that had taken place here. The air was thick with dread, and Daniel felt like he was wading through a dark swamp. In the centre of the room stood an old wooden bed. Legends spoke of a spirit that was chained to the bed, a spirit that would pull anyone who dared sleep on it into the netherworld.

Suddenly, the bed's chains rattled violently. Daniel could see a figure, bound and struggling, reaching out to him, its fingers brushing his ankle. The touch was ice-cold, causing a sharp pain that shot up his leg.

Terrified, he bolted towards the exit, but the inn's layout seemed to have changed. Hallways stretched endlessly, and rooms shifted. He was trapped in a never-ending maze.

Mrs. Gray's voice echoed through the walls, "You were warned..."

He finally stumbled into the main hall, where Mrs. Gray stood, her eyes no longer kind but dark and hollow. She seemed to float, her feet barely touching the ground. Behind her, the spirits of the inn materialized. The bishop, the children, the sacrificed souls, all staring at him with pleading eyes.

"You wished to capture our stories," Mrs. Gray's voice was a distorted chorus, the voices of all the spirits speaking in unison, "Now, you shall become a part of them."

The spirits lunged at him, their cold hands pulling him into the darkness. The last thing Daniel saw was the inn's ancient wooden door slamming shut.

Weeks later, another traveller came by the Ancient Ram Inn, drawn by tales of its haunting beauty. The innkeeper, Mrs. Emilia Gray, welcomed him with a gentle smile. The traveller noticed a new photograph adorning the inn's wall. It was of a man, his face twisted in terror, with shadows of figures looming behind him.

"He was the last one who tried to capture our stories," Mrs. Gray whispered, her eyes gleaming with a malevolent light.

CHAPTER 9:

The Princes in the Tower

The Tower of London had seen many a cruel fate meted out within its cold walls. From traitors to nobles, from the innocent to the schemers, countless souls had breathed their last under its watchful turrets. But none evoked more sorrow and mystery than the two young princes, Edward and Richard.

Cassie leaned against the old stones, taking in the Tower with a sense of foreboding. She had travelled from America, inspired by the ancient stories that were sewn into Britain's fabric. An amateur historian, she was drawn most to the story of the princes who had vanished without a trace.

A dense fog rolled in from the Thames, its tendrils wrapping around the tower and dimming the last of the evening light. Cassie felt a shiver, though not from the cold. There was an electric charge in the air, a buzz that hinted at energies long dormant.

She'd managed to arrange a night alone in the Tower. A hefty donation to the preservation fund and a connection or two had helped. The guards had looked at her with a mix of admiration and pity. The stories of night-time spectres had turned even the boldest hearts away. But Cassie was determined.

With a torch in hand, she walked the narrow corridors of the Tower. The silence was unsettling, broken only by her echoing footsteps. She made her way to the chamber where it was believed the princes were held.

It was a small room, more a cell, with narrow windows that let in little light. The room was stark, save for two small beds. Cassie could almost hear the whispered conversations between two brothers, uncertain and afraid.

She set up her recording equipment and sat in the centre of the room. The hours ticked by. Midnight approached, and the atmosphere shifted palpably. A cold breeze flowed through the room, making the flames of her candles dance frantically.

Suddenly, the faint sound of crying reached her ears. It grew louder, a mournful, heart-wrenching sound. Then another joined in, two children weeping in the dark. Cassie strained her eyes, and in the dim light, she saw them. Two spectral figures, translucent and blue, huddled together.

"Edward, will they come for us?" the younger one, presumably Richard, whimpered.

The elder prince tried to console him, "Hush, Richard. All will be well."

As Cassie watched, unable to tear her eyes away, the chamber's wooden door creaked open slowly. A shadowy figure loomed in the doorway, darker than the night, an essence of pure malevolence. The princes clung to each other, their ghostly forms quivering.

Cassie wanted to scream, to run, but she was paralyzed, a mere spectator to the tragic replay of history.

The figure approached, his face obscured by the hood of his cloak. As he neared the princes, his hand, skeletal and rotting, emerged from the cloak, holding a pillow. The air grew thick with tension and fear.

Edward, ever the protector, stood in front of Richard, his young frame shaking but defiant. "Stay away from us!" he cried out.

The shadow didn't respond. It lunged at Edward, the pillow descending. Cassie watched in horror as the scene played out. The younger prince's cries were stifled soon after.

The room grew darker, if that was even possible, and the temperature dropped further. Cassie felt a hand on her shoulder. Whipping around, she came face to face with the hooded spectre, its face still hidden in shadows.

She screamed, pushing herself away, scrambling to her feet, and running for the door. But the Tower's labyrinthine corridors twisted and turned, leading her further into its depths. The heavy fog outside had seeped in, and she felt like she was running through a nightmare.

Behind her, the echoing footsteps of the shadowy figure pursued her. The cries of the princes still rang in her ears, a haunting lament.

As she ran, other spirits of the Tower manifested. Headless apparitions, spectral guards, and mournful ladies in waiting, each with their tales of woe. But none were as relentless as the hooded spectre.

Cassie stumbled into the chapel of St. John, thinking she'd find solace there. But the chapel was filled with the spirits of those executed in the Tower, all kneeling in prayer, their translucent forms glowing softly.

In the centre stood a priest, his hands raised in blessing. But his eyes... they were empty voids of darkness. He turned to Cassie, pointing a bony finger at her. "You bear witness," he intoned.

Behind her, the hooded figure entered, the chapel's doors slamming shut with a resounding boom. Cassie felt herself being drawn toward the altar, her limbs no longer under her control. The ghosts chanted in unison, a haunting dirge that echoed the sorrow of centuries.

The hooded figure approached, and as he drew closer, he pulled back his hood. But there was no face, only darkness, an abyss that seemed to pull Cassie in. She felt herself falling, descending into the depths of the Tower's history, every soul, every story entwining around her.

When the guards opened the Tower the next morning, they found Cassie's equipment in the princes' chamber. But of Cassie, there was no sign. The Tower had claimed another soul, another story to add to its dark tapestry.

And on some nights, when the fog rolls in thick and heavy, you can hear the cries of the princes, the chants of the chapel's spirits, and now, the terrified scream of an

American tourist who ventured too close to the heart of the Tower's darkness.

CHAPTER 10:

Lady Lovibond

Trevor had always been drawn to the sea. Since his early childhood, the ocean's vastness and mystery called to him. His father had told tales of the sea, of monstrous creatures and ships that vanished, never to be seen again. But one story always sent shivers down his spine — the legend of the Lady Lovibond.

A native of Kent, Trevor was familiar with the stories about the Goodwin Sands, a treacherous stretch of sandbanks off the coast, which had claimed many ships over the years. And among those ships was the Lady Lovibond.

As legend had it, in 1748, on the 13th of February, the Lady Lovibond set sail as a celebration of Captain Simon Reed's wedding. But jealousy and betrayal lay hidden beneath the deck. In a fit of jealous rage, the first mate, Rivers, who secretly loved the captain's bride, Annetta, struck the captain unconscious and steered the ship into the Sands. The ship and all its passengers met a watery grave.

It was said that every fifty years, the ghost ship reappeared, a spectral sight cruising the waters, reliving its last moments.

As luck would have it, the 300th anniversary of the Lady Lovibond's sinking was just days away. An amateur marine archaeologist, Trevor felt this was the chance of a lifetime. He wanted to witness and document the phenomenon. Armed with modern recording equipment, he rented a boat and sailed out, anchoring near the Goodwin Sands.

The day was gloomy, with thick, heavy clouds that blocked the sunlight. The sea was eerily calm, the waves just gentle caresses against his boat. As the evening wore on, a dense fog began to roll in, reducing visibility to mere meters.

The boat's old radio crackled to life, an ancient tune playing softly, one that Trevor didn't recognize. It sounded like a mournful love song from centuries past. The temperature dropped suddenly, and he could see his breath in the air, even though it was a relatively warm February.

He glanced at his watch. Almost midnight.

Then, from the fog, a silhouette emerged. It was a ship, grand and majestic, but with an aura of melancholy. The Lady Lovibond. She looked as if she was still in her prime, sails billowing, her wooden deck gleaming. Lanterns illuminated her, casting an otherworldly glow.

Trevor quickly began documenting, his cameras capturing the spectral vision. He could see ghostly figures on deck, dancing to a silent tune. And there, at the helm, stood Captain Reed, his lovely bride Annetta by his side. But lurking in the shadows was Rivers, his face twisted in anger and despair.

As the ship glided silently, Trevor felt an inexplicable urge. He needed to be on that ship. Before he knew it, he was in his dinghy, rowing towards the ghostly vessel. As he got closer, the soft strains of music became audible, a haunting melody that tugged at his heart.

He boarded the ship, his feet touching the solid, yet misty deck. The apparitions paid him no mind, lost in their eternal celebration. He approached the captain and Annetta, who were dancing, lost in each other's eyes. But as he neared them, Annetta's eyes suddenly met his. They were deep, endless pools of sorrow.

She whispered, her voice echoing like it was coming from far away, "Save us."

Confused, Trevor turned to look at Rivers, who was now approaching with a menacing look. The world around Trevor began to spin, the music growing louder and more frantic. The ship started tilting, and water began flooding the deck.

He tried to run, to get back to his boat, but the water was swift, pulling him under. He struggled, gasping for breath, but the weight of the water was too much. As he sank, he saw the ship begin to break apart, the apparitions fading away, their cries of despair echoing in his ears.

When the sun rose, the fog had lifted, and the sea was calm once again. Trevor's empty boat floated aimlessly, the recording equipment still running. And if one were to play back the footage, they'd see the ghostly Lady Lovibond, her passengers forever trapped in their final moments, and a new addition to their ranks – a young man with terror in his eyes, forever bound to the ship's tragic fate.

CHAPTER 11:

The Screaming Spectres of Fyvie Castle

Anna had always had an insatiable curiosity about the paranormal, a trait she probably inherited from her grandmother, a famous Scottish medium. When she heard stories about Fyvie Castle, nestled deep in Aberdeenshire, she knew she had to visit. Locals whispered tales of tragic women whose restless spirits still haunted the castle, their screams echoing through its halls.

Anna booked a night's stay in the castle, which had been converted into a luxurious hotel. The dark, stone walls towered above her as she approached, an intimidating and imposing structure that looked like it had been plucked straight from a gothic novel.

"Miss MacDonald," greeted the concierge, a petite woman with a tight bun and pinched features. "We've prepared the Green Room for you."

Anna paused. The Green Room was said to be the most haunted room in the castle, its name derived from the eerie luminescence that guests claimed to have seen during the night. She nodded, swallowing her unease, reminding herself that this was precisely what she had come for.

The room was grand, with opulent furnishings and a massive four-poster bed. Anna set up her equipment: voice recorders, cameras, and EMF meters. If there were spirits in this castle, she would find proof of them.

Night fell, and the castle seemed to come alive. Shadows danced on the walls, and every creak of the wood and whistle of the wind seemed magnified. Anna lay on the bed, the dim glow from her equipment illuminating the room.

The castle was silent until, out of the stillness, a soft sob echoed. Anna sat upright, her heart racing. The sobbing grew louder, taking on a desperate, haunting quality. It seemed to come from the corridor outside.

Anna followed the sound, her camera in hand. The sobs led her to a portrait of a beautiful, raven-haired woman. Her eyes were sorrowful, and her lips seemed to quiver, as if she were on the verge of crying.

Anna felt a cold hand touch her shoulder. Whirling around, there was no one there. But the room had grown colder, and the air was thick with despair. Suddenly, a piercing scream tore through the castle, so loud that Anna had to cover her ears. But even then, it was deafening.

The scream seemed to emanate from all directions, bouncing off the stone walls. As it continued, other voices joined in – a cacophony of terror and agony. Anna could hear words now. "Save us. Release us."

Panicking, Anna dashed back to the Green Room, but the door wouldn't budge. The screams intensified, so loud that the room seemed to vibrate with their energy. She could see apparitions now – three women, all in various states of distress.

One had ropes binding her hands, another was cloaked in a wedding dress, her face pale and twisted in horror, and the third was the woman from the portrait, her beautiful features distorted in agony.

The three spirits converged on Anna, their hands reaching for her. She could feel their cold fingers grazing her skin, their pain and sorrow seeping into her. Their eyes, full of centuries of torment, locked onto hers.

Unable to bear it, Anna screamed, a guttural sound of pure terror.

The next morning, the concierge, accompanied by a few concerned staff, finally managed to break down the door to the Green Room. Anna lay on the floor, her eyes wide open, staring at something none of them could see. Her equipment was scattered everywhere, recordings still running.

Later, when the recordings were played, amidst the static and ambient noise, one could hear the haunting sobs, the terrifying screams, and Anna's voice, barely a whisper, saying, "I see you. I understand."

The Green Room was closed off after that, but staff and guests still claimed to hear the sorrowful sobs and chilling screams echoing in the castle corridors. And sometimes, they'd hear a new voice, softly whispering amidst the screams – a voice that sounded eerily like Anna's.

CHAPTER 12:

The Glastonbury Abbey Monks

Leonard had never considered himself to be a religious man. To him, stone and mortar were just that, nothing divine about them. But when he inherited a vast estate from a distant relative, which included the ruins of Glastonbury Abbey, he couldn't resist a visit. History had always fascinated him. After all, what's more exciting than the tales of kings and conspiracies, of deaths and betrayals?

The ruins, mostly stone walls and fragments of arches, lay on vast grounds that were overgrown and wild. It was said to be one of the oldest Christian monasteries in England, with tales of it being connected to King Arthur and his fabled Avalon.

Leonard strolled around the ruins, occasionally touching the moss-covered stones, trying to connect with a past long gone. The sun began to set, casting eerie shadows through the broken arches and crumbling walls. It was a serene picture, the remains of the abbey bathed in an orange-red glow.

However, as daylight faded, the atmosphere shifted. The air became cold, and Leonard could feel an oppressive weight pushing down on him. It felt as though the ruins were not happy with his presence. Shivering, he tried to shake off the feeling, attributing it to the descending darkness.

That's when he heard it – a soft, rhythmic chanting that seemed to be coming from beneath the ground. Leonard knelt and pressed his ear to the cold stone. The chanting was clearer now, words in Latin, the soft whispers of monks in prayer. Trying to rationalize it, he thought it might be some sort of echo from the past. The land was known to play tricks on the mind.

Suddenly, a gust of wind blew, and the entire abbey lit up with ghostly light. Transparent figures in monk's robes appeared, walking the grounds, their heads bowed in prayer. Their lips moved, but no sound came out. Leonard, paralyzed with fear, hid behind a wall, peering out to observe the spectral procession.

One of the monks, distinguishable by his higher rank, perhaps an abbot, paused and turned his head towards Leonard's hiding place. Their eyes locked. The ghostly figure's eyes were pits of darkness, yet they seemed to be searching Leonard's soul.

Leonard felt a pull, an urge to join the procession, to walk with them in eternal prayer. He felt his feet moving of their own accord, stepping out from his hiding spot and moving closer to the group. He could hear the chants clearly now, the hauntingly beautiful melody calling him.

The abbot extended a cold, spectral hand. Leonard, still in a trance, was about to take it when a hand gripped his shoulder, yanking him back. A voice whispered urgently in his ear, "Do not join them!"

Leonard was pulled into the shadows, and the spectral procession faded as suddenly as it had appeared. Gasping for breath, he turned to see a hooded figure beside him. The hood was lowered to reveal an old woman, her eyes sharp and knowing.

"Who are you?" Leonard croaked.

"I've been watching over this abbey for years," she replied. "I'm the guardian. Those monks... they're trapped in a loop of their last moments. The Abbey was desecrated, you see. They're praying for salvation, but it's a prayer that's never answered."

"Why did they try to pull me in?"

"Their number dwindles as time goes by," she whispered. "They try to replace their ranks, pulling in unsuspecting souls. Had you taken his hand, you'd be one of them, forever trapped."

Leonard, shaken, took a moment to process the gravity of what had just occurred. "How do I thank you?"

She looked at him intently. "By leaving and never returning. This ground isn't meant for the living anymore."

Leonard needed no further prompting. He left the abbey and never looked back.

However, the tale doesn't end there. Leonard, although safe from the clutches of the eternal procession, was forever marked by that night. He began to hear the chants, softly at first, but growing louder, always in the dead of night. No matter where he went, the prayers of the monks haunted him.

One night, overwhelmed and desperate for silence, Leonard ventured into the woods near his home. The full moon shone down, illuminating his path. The chants grew louder, more insistent. Ahead, in a clearing, stood the spectral abbot, his hand outstretched.

Leonard, tears streaming down his face, whispered, "I understand now."

He took the abbot's hand, and the woods fell silent.

Residents say that on moonlit nights, if you venture into those woods, you can hear the soft chants of monks. And among them is a voice, newer than the rest, forever trapped between the realms of the living and the dead.

CHAPTER 13:

The Ghostly Piper of Duntrune Castle

On a jagged cliff overlooking the Scottish coastline, Duntrune Castle stood as a silent sentinel. Built in the 12th century, its history was intertwined with legends of bloodshed, betrayal, and heartbreak. One legend in particular has echoed through time: the haunting sounds of the Ghostly Piper.

Helen MacGregor, an aspiring musician from Glasgow, had been drawn to the legend ever since she was a child. When she was offered a summer residency at Duntrune Castle to work on her compositions, she couldn't resist. An old friend of the family, Lord Duntrune, had generously extended the invitation.

"It'll be peaceful," he'd said with a wry smile, "if you don't mind a bit of piping in the evening."

Helen had laughed it off, attributing the story to the wild imaginations of the locals. Yet, on her first night, as twilight faded into the inky darkness of a Scottish evening, she heard it - the distant, haunting melody of bagpipes echoing through the castle's stone corridors.

Curiosity piqued, Helen followed the sound, leading her to the castle's old tower. The closer she got, the clearer the melody became, a mournful tune full of sorrow. Yet, upon reaching the top, she found the room empty, the last notes lingering in the air before dissipating into silence.

Shaken, Helen spoke to Lord Duntrune the next morning, "Was it you playing the bagpipes last night?"

He looked at her, surprise evident in his eyes. "I haven't played in years," he replied. "But I told you about our piper, didn't I?"

Over breakfast, he shared the tale. Centuries ago, during one of the countless clan skirmishes that marked Scottish history, a piper had been taken captive in Duntrune Castle. He was imprisoned in the tower where he'd play his pipes to communicate with his clan across the waters, letting them know he was still alive. However, as a form of psychological torture, his captors cut off his hands, ensuring he'd never play again. Days later, the piper died, but his spirit, it seemed, was not ready to leave.

"I've tried to make peace with him," Lord Duntrune said with a sigh. "But he plays, every night, without fail."

For some reason, Helen felt a connection to the piper, a fellow musician torn away from his passion. Night after night, she'd sit in the tower, listening to the ghostly melodies, tears streaming down her face. She began to document the tunes, incorporating them into her compositions.

One evening, as the last notes faded, Helen felt a cold gust of wind. In the dim light, she saw a shadowy figure, a man in tattered clothing, his hands a mangled mess. He looked at her, his eyes pools of endless sorrow.

"Play," he whispered, his voice echoing through the chamber.

Terrified, yet compelled, Helen picked up her violin and began to play, matching the piper's haunting melody. The figure seemed to sway, lost in the music, and for a brief moment, there was a connection, a shared understanding between two souls bound by their love for music.

As dawn approached, the figure faded, leaving Helen exhausted but exhilarated. She felt she'd found her muse.

Yet, the next night, the piper's tune turned desperate, frantic. The shadowy figure appeared once again, this time closer, his mangled hands reaching out for her.

"Play," he demanded, his voice echoing louder.

Helen, trembling, picked up her violin, but the notes were off, the melody twisted. The figure grew angrier, the room colder.

"You must play right," he hissed, his face inches from hers.

The weeks that followed were a torment for Helen. Each night, the piper demanded she play, and each time she faltered, his wrath intensified. The once-beautiful melodies turned dark, reflecting the piper's descent into madness. Helen grew gaunt, her once vibrant eyes now hollow from fear.

Lord Duntrune, concerned for her well-being, urged her to leave. "The castle, it's not safe," he whispered. "The piper, he's claimed souls before."

But Helen couldn't. The music, the connection she'd felt, kept her rooted. She believed she could free the piper, give him the peace he so desperately sought.

On her last night, Helen made a decision. She sat in the tower, waiting for the ghostly apparition. When he appeared, his presence more menacing than ever, she spoke, her voice firm.

"I will play one last time, but you must let me go."

The piper, hesitating, finally nodded.

Helen played, pouring all her emotions into the melody, her sorrow, her fear, her empathy for the lost soul before her. The notes flowed, pure and untainted, filling the room with an ethereal light. The shadowy figure seemed to absorb the light, his form becoming more defined, the anger in his eyes replaced by gratitude.

As the final notes lingered, Helen watched as the piper played one last time, his melody merging with hers, before dissipating into the dawn light.

Exhausted, Helen lay down, her heart at peace. But the next morning, she was found lifeless, her violin by her side, a serene expression on her face.

Lord Duntrune, heartbroken, closed off the tower. But locals say, on some nights, when the moon is high, you can hear two melodies echoing from Duntrune Castle - a piper and a violinist, their souls forever entwined in a haunting dance.

CHAPTER 14:

The Ghostly Soldiers of Edgehill

A driving rain battered the small inn, a structure that had once been a farmhouse before being converted into a place of rest for weary travellers. The "Bloody Horse Inn," it was ironically named, situated near the Edgehill battlefield in Warwickshire. An old battleground, the site had been the theatre of a fierce engagement during the English Civil War.

Now, decades after the guns and canons had fallen silent, the inn stood as the sole witness to those tragic events. Inside, the fireplace roared, offering warmth to the handful of patrons seeking shelter from the inclement weather.

Walter, the innkeeper, a burly man with a long beard, regaled tales of the historic battlefield to anyone who'd listen. Tonight's listeners were Tom, a young lad traveling with his sister Clara, and an old man known only as Mr. Grey, a local who often spent his evenings at the inn.

"It's said that on nights like this, you can still hear the soldiers," Walter began, his eyes glinting with a mixture of fear and excitement. "Not just their voices, mind you. But the clang of swords, the shouts of commanders, the whinnying of horses."

Tom snorted, "Nonsense."

Clara, however, shushed her brother. "Let him tell the story, Tom."

Mr. Grey sipped his ale, saying nothing, his eyes distant, as if he was lost in a memory.

"As the tale goes," Walter continued, "two local farm boys, curious as ever, decided to camp out on the battlefield one evening, determined to debunk the myths. They laughed, drank, and settled into their tents. But come midnight, the air grew cold, and a thick fog enveloped the land. From the mist, the unmistakable sound of battle cries emerged."

Walter paused for effect, enjoying the rapt attention he was receiving.

"The boys, terrified, dared not leave their tents. They clung to each other, listening to the sounds of an ancient battle play out right outside. It felt...real. The ground vibrated with the march of phantom feet, spectral horses galloped past, and invisible swords clashed in deadly duels. The night was alive with the echoes of war."

Tom rolled his eyes but said nothing, though Clara's face was pale. She whispered, "What happened to the boys?"

Walter leaned in closer. "Morning found their abandoned campsite. Tents torn, belongings scattered. But of the boys? No trace was ever found. Just a pair of boots, filled to the brim with fresh blood."

Mr. Grey cleared his throat, interrupting the morbid tale. "This isn't just a story, young ones. I knew those boys. Played with them when we were but children. The battlefield took them, and they've never been seen since."

Clara's eyes widened, while Tom, usually sceptical, seemed unnerved.

Night deepened outside, and the rain showed no signs of letting up. The inn's guests decided it would be safer to stay the night. Walter, sensing an opportunity, offered them rooms.

As Clara and Tom made their way to their respective rooms, Clara hesitated. "Tom, do you believe the story?"

Tom hesitated, then whispered, "Stay in your room tonight, Clara. Just in case."

The night was restless. The storm outside mirrored the turmoil inside the inn. Clara, cocooned in her bed, was jerked awake by a chilling scream. Jumping out of bed, she raced to Tom's room.

But he wasn't there.

Panicking, she dashed downstairs to find Walter and Mr. Grey in a heated discussion.

"They shouldn't have stayed," Mr. Grey was saying. "The battlefield calls out on nights like this."

Walter looked pale. "I thought it was just a story."

Ignoring them, Clara cried out, "Tom's gone!"

Mr. Grey turned to her, his face grim. "Then he's on the battlefield."

Without waiting, Clara ran out into the storm, the rain blinding her, the mud pulling at her feet. But she could hear it — the distant sounds of battle, growing louder with every step.

In the thick of the fog, shapes began to materialize — soldiers in worn-out armour, spectral horses, and ghostly figures locked in eternal combat. Among them, she spotted Tom, dazed, wandering amidst the phantoms.

Clara raced to him, pulling him away from a ghostly cavalier who was charging in their direction. Together, they tried to find their way back to the inn. But the mist was disorienting. Every turn took them deeper into the heart of the spectral battle.

Suddenly, a phantom soldier, his face half-rotted but eyes burning with fury, lunged at Tom, thrusting a ghostly sword through him. Tom screamed, collapsing into Clara's arms, his body becoming ethereal, merging with the fog.

"No!" Clara screamed, tears mingling with the rain. The last thing she saw before fainting was the ghostly soldier dragging Tom away into the mist.

Morning found Clara, unconscious, at the edge of the battlefield. Walter and Mr. Grey, with a search party, had been scouring the area for hours.

Clara awoke with a start, the horrors of the night flooding back. "Tom..." she sobbed.

Mr. Grey, his face full of sorrow, whispered, "The battlefield has claimed another."

Days turned into weeks, and weeks into months. Tom was never found. Clara, a broken shadow of herself, would often be seen at the edge of the battlefield, whispering her brother's name, hoping against hope.

Legend had it that on stormy nights, if you listened closely, you could hear a new voice among the spectral soldiers, a young voice, calling out in the darkness: "Clara?"

And from afar, an answering cry: "Tom!"

The battle at Edgehill, it seemed, was destined to rage on forever, its victims forever trapped in its ghostly grip.

CHAPTER 15:

The Restless Souls of the Mary Rose

The Mary Rose was an exemplar of maritime mastery. She was one of the foremost warships of the Tudor navy, named after King Henry VIII's favourite sister. On a fateful day in 1545, during a battle against the French fleet, the mighty Mary Rose sank, taking with her hundreds of souls.

The ship rested undisturbed at the bottom of the Solent, near Portsmouth, for over four centuries until she was discovered and raised in 1982. A marvel of its time, the resurrected ship was meticulously conserved and displayed at the Mary Rose Museum, attracting thousands of tourists from all over the world.

However, as with most artifacts that come with a history, there were tales that clung to the timber and rigging of the Mary Rose. Some said that the souls of the drowned men still lingered around the ship. Museum staff whispered of phantom footsteps, echoing voices from the past, and an ever-present chill that had nothing to do with air conditioning.

Sophie, an archaeology student with an affinity for the supernatural, had always been drawn to the Mary Rose. When the opportunity arose for her to intern at the museum, she was overjoyed. The old ship intrigued her, not just for its historical significance but the ghostly tales that surrounded it. Sophie wanted to be close to the ship, to hear her stories and, if fortunate, witness a spectral sailor or two.

Her first day at the museum was a whirlwind of introductions and briefings. As night approached, the museum's supervisor, Mr. Thompson, a grizzled old man with a penchant for chewing tobacco, had one last piece of advice: "Stay away from the ship after dark. She don't like it."

Sophie smiled, attributing his warning to the tales that floated around. But Mr. Thompson's eyes, earnest and a tad fearful, told her he was serious.

That night, curiosity getting the better of her, Sophie decided to stay late. Armed with a flashlight, she entered the dimly lit chamber housing the remains of the Mary Rose. The ship stood there, grand and imposing, its dark timbers and skeletal frame casting eerie shadows.

Sophie felt a chill, but she pressed on, her flashlight beam dancing across the ship's remnants. The silence was palpable, interrupted only by the occasional drip of water from the ship's timbers. Suddenly, a sound caught her ear—a soft humming, echoing through the chamber. The voice was mournful, filled with a sadness that transcended time. Sophie's heart raced as she followed the sound, which seemed to emanate from the bowels of the ship.

Deep within the ship's lower decks, the humming grew louder, accompanied by whispers and the creak of ropes.

The air grew colder, each breath visible in the dim light. Sophie's flashlight revealed a ghostly figure—a sailor, dressed in Tudor garb, his face pale and eyes vacant.

The sailor didn't notice her. Instead, he was busy working, securing phantom ropes and adjusting non-existent sails. Around him, other spectres moved—men caught in the daily routines of a ship long sunken.

Suddenly, one of the figures turned to face Sophie, his eyes hollow but filled with an accusatory glare. Sophie gasped and stumbled backward. The ghosts' movements became frantic, their whispers turning to anguished cries. The sailor who had noticed her pointed, and a chorus of ghostly voices rang out, "Intruder! Intruder!"

Terrified, Sophie turned to run, but her path was blocked by more spectral sailors, their faces twisted in anger and despair. They reached for her, their ghostly fingers icy cold. She was trapped.

A loud clang echoed through the chamber, and the apparitions vanished. Gasping for breath, Sophie found herself alone in the bowels of the Mary Rose. From the entrance, the beam of another flashlight approached, and Mr. Thompson's voice called out, "I told you to stay away after dark!"

He helped Sophie to her feet, his eyes filled with concern. "They don't mean harm," he said softly. "But they're trapped, reliving their last moments over and over. They get agitated when the living disturb them."

Sophie, shaken, nodded. "I... I just wanted to see if the tales were true."

Mr. Thompson sighed. "The ship has a way of drawing people in. But we must respect the souls that are trapped here. They deserve peace."

Sophie agreed, and from that day, she never ventured near the ship after dark. However, every now and then, when she was alone in the museum, she'd hear a soft humming or the distant sound of ropes creaking. A chilling reminder of the restless souls aboard the Mary Rose.

The ship, a marvel of history, continued to attract thousands. But those who worked closely with her knew better than to linger after dark. For within her timbers and below her decks, the souls of the drowned men still toiled, waiting for the day they would finally find peace.

CHAPTER 16:

The Ghosts of Naseby Battlefield

In the picturesque landscapes of Northamptonshire, a history of violence has left scars deeper than any plow could etch. The Naseby Battlefield saw the clash of Royalists and Parliamentarians in one of the decisive battles of the English Civil War. The bloody conflict, which took place in 1645, led to thousands of men losing their lives. And as with many places stained by death, some spirits were unable to move on.

David Jenkins, an aspiring writer, moved into a cottage near the battlefield. He wanted isolation, hoping the serenity would coax out his next bestseller. His neighbours, Mr. and Mrs. Thompson, were pleasant, older folks, living a couple of miles away. They welcomed him with fresh pie and, as the sun set, a cryptic warning.

"Nighttime walks might not be the best idea, especially near the battlefield," Mrs. Thompson said, her wrinkled eyes narrowing.

David chuckled, "Afraid I'll trip over some history?"

Mr. Thompson's voice was grave. "It's not the history underfoot that's of concern; it's the history that still marches."

David thought little of it. He attributed their words to local superstitions, perhaps a tad too much brandy. However, that night, as David settled into his new bed, he heard it: the distant thud of drums. They were slow and rhythmic, the kind of beat that pulls you into its cadence. Curiosity piqued, David stepped outside.

The cool night air was heavy with mist, making it difficult to see much. But the drumbeat was unmistakable, growing louder. He strained his eyes, and through the fog, he saw what looked like ghostly apparitions of soldiers, their transparent figures illuminated by the glow of spectral lanterns. They seemed locked in combat, their phantom weapons clashing with echoing clangs that belied their insubstantial nature.

Heart pounding, David retreated indoors, locking the door behind him. The ghostly tableau continued outside. The chilling screams of dying men filled the night, punctuated by the mournful cries of lost souls. David spent the night huddled under blankets, praying for dawn.

The next morning, the scene was clear, as if the battle had never taken place. Yet the ground felt colder, and there was an air of heaviness, like the world was holding its breath.

David decided to pay the Thompsons a visit, hoping for an explanation. The couple seemed unsurprised by his tale.

"You've seen the phantom reenactment," Mr. Thompson began. "Every so often, the spirits rise to replay that fateful day. They're bound to the land, restless and lost."

"But why?" David asked, his writer's mind eager for a story.

Mrs. Thompson sighed. "Some say it's because of the sheer violence and hatred of that day. Others believe there's something in the soil, a curse or malevolence, that binds them here."

David was both terrified and fascinated. That night, and the nights following, he sat by his window, documenting the ghostly reenactments. He noted the strategies, the faces of the generals, and the soldiers who fell. He began to recognize the repeated deaths of certain soldiers, their spectral forms fading only to rise and die again.

Then, one night, as David watched, a soldier seemed to notice him. The soldier, a young man with a bloodied bandana around his head, stared directly at David, pointing at him. The scene around the young soldier continued its repetitive cycle, but he remained still, his gaze never leaving David.

The following day, a heavy fog enveloped the area. David stepped outside, and the young soldier from the night before stood there, his translucent figure clearer in daylight. David froze, staring at the apparition. The ghost spoke, his voice echoing as if from a great distance, "You've been watching us."

David gulped, managing a nod. "I'm a writer. I was documenting..."

The ghost interrupted, "We are trapped, forced to relive our last day. But you... you can free us."

David blinked. "How?"

The apparition extended a hand. "Join us. Become one of us."

The chill of realization hit David. He took a step back, but the ghostly soldier advanced. "You've seen our pain. Help us."

David turned to run, but the fog thickened, obscuring his vision. Ghostly hands reached out, grasping at him. He could hear the cries of the trapped souls, their desperation palpable. They weren't malicious, just desperate for release.

David tried to fend them off, but there were too many. The hands pulled him down, and the world went dark.

The next morning, the Thompsons found a note on David's door. It simply read, "Tell my story."

And so, the legend of the Naseby Battlefield grew. Locals spoke of the writer who joined the ranks of the spectral army. They said that on certain nights, you could see him, notepad in hand, forever documenting the eternal battle. The once-silent soldiers now had a voice, and their cries of pain and desperation became tales told in hushed tones, a chilling reminder of history's grip on the present.

CHAPTER 17:

The Cursed Skull of Bettiscombe Manor

The winding lanes of West Dorset hid secrets that few could fathom. The rolling greens and serene pastures of the county were deceptive, for the shadows of ancient evils lurked underneath. And nowhere was this more apparent than in the village of Bettiscombe, home to the historic Bettiscombe Manor.

Raina had always been drawn to tales of the unknown. A historian by profession and a ghost-hunter by passion, she had travelled to the most haunted spots in Britain. But Bettiscombe was different. Here, it wasn't just a wandering spirit or a forlorn apparition; it was the sinister story of a cursed skull.

The legend was a tale passed down through generations. The manor had been home to the Pinney family for centuries. One of the Pinneys, during a trip to the West Indies, had acquired a slave named Azibo. When Azibo fell gravely ill, his dying wish was to be buried back in his homeland. But after his death, the family, ignoring his plea, buried him in the local cemetery.

Soon after, terrifying incidents began. Tormented wails echoed through the manor at night. Objects moved on their own, and dark shadows flitted across rooms. Most unnerving was the skull, which, no matter where it was buried, always found its way back to the house. It was said to be Azibo's, restless and angered. Eventually, the skull was given a place in the house, and the disturbances lessened, but they never truly stopped.

Raina had come prepared, having read all there was on the manor. She had secured permission to stay a night, determined to experience and perhaps communicate with the spirit of Azibo. Her equipment, including EMF meters, voice recorders, and infrared cameras, was set up in the room where the skull was kept.

The room was gloomy, its walls lined with ancestral portraits whose eyes seemed to follow her every move. But dominating the space was a glass case on a wooden pedestal. Inside, the skull sat, its hollow eyes seeming to look right through her.

As night fell, Raina started her vigil. She attempted to communicate, asking Azibo if he was present. Hours went by with no activity. The quiet of the house was deafening.

Around midnight, Raina decided to take a break, heading to the small kitchen to make herself a cup of tea. But as she turned, she stopped in her tracks. From the hallway, she could hear a faint humming, a tune both sorrowful and haunting. Following the sound, she realized it was emanating from the room with the skull.

She slowly entered, her heart pounding. The room was cold, the temperature having dropped drastically. And there, next to the glass case, stood a figure, transparent but unmistakable. It was a man, his features African, his attire reminiscent of the slaves from the West Indies. His eyes were closed, lost in his tune, but as he felt Raina's presence, they opened, locking onto her with an intensity that sent shivers down her spine.

Raina tried to speak, her voice barely a whisper. "Azibo?"

The figure nodded. The room grew colder, the sorrow in his eyes deepening. He approached her, his form slightly flickering like an old television with bad reception.

"I wish to rest," he murmured, his voice echoing, filled with pain. "My homeland... I must return."

Raina, though terrified, felt a deep sympathy. "I want to help. Tell me what to do."

But Azibo shook his head. "Too many years, too much anger. The land here is cursed by my pain. It won't let me leave. But you... you can join me."

Before Raina could react, the room changed. She was no longer in the manor. Instead, she found herself amidst a vast sugarcane plantation. The sun was cruel, beating down on the workers who toiled, their chains clinking with every move. She felt the weight on her own ankles, the heat, the suffocating despair.

She spotted Azibo, young and strong, but with the same sorrowful eyes. He was beckoning her. "See my pain," he whispered.

Time seemed to twist and turn. Night fell, and Raina found herself back in the room, but not alone. All around her, ghostly figures from various eras stood, their eyes empty, souls trapped by the curse.

"You're not the first to try and help," a voice beside her said. It was a young man, dressed in a WWI uniform, a tag around his neck reading 'Lt. Charles Howard'. "I too wanted to set things right. But the curse is strong."

Raina, panic rising, realized her peril. The curse didn't just want to keep Azibo; it hungered for more souls. She had to break it.

Rushing to the case, she took the skull, ignoring the cacophony of voices that rose around her. The whispers grew louder, turning into screams, the room spinning.

Using all her strength, Raina chanted every purification ritual she knew. The atmosphere grew thick, the pressure immense. But as dawn broke, a blinding light filled the room, and Raina felt herself being thrown back.

When she came to, the manor was silent. The oppressive air had lifted. The skull, still in her hand, now seemed just that—a skull. The curse, it seemed, was broken.

Relief washed over Raina. She had done it. But as she got up, a sharp pain coursed through her body. Looking down, she saw her hands—they were old, wrinkled. Racing to a mirror, she was met with the face of an elderly woman staring back.

The curse was broken, but at a cost. Time, it seemed, had taken its toll.

Raina lived out her days in the village, growing older by the day, her youth the price paid for meddling with forces beyond comprehension. She passed away a week later, a century lived in mere days.

And while Bettiscombe Manor stood silent, free from its haunting, the villagers often spoke of seeing an old woman wandering its halls, whispering tales of a cursed skull and lost time.

CHAPTER 18:

The White Lady of Avenham Park, Preston

Avenham Park, with its lush green expanses and picturesque views of the River Ribble, was a haven for the people of Preston. But when the sun dipped below the horizon, and a hush fell over the land, a shadow emerged from the annals of history – a figure known only as the White Lady.

David Holt, a journalist from Manchester, had heard the whispers. A woman in white, appearing at twilight, floating across the park. Her origin was a mystery, but the locals knew one thing – those who gazed upon her directly seldom returned to tell the tale.

Armed with a healthy scepticism, David decided to unravel this tale. It was the month of October, and the wind carried with it an unspoken chill. As the sun bid its farewell, David stationed himself on a bench overlooking the river, his trusty camera at his side. He was ready to debunk this legend.

The clock ticked by. An hour. Then two. Just as David's resolve began to wane, a soft humming reached his ears. The atmosphere changed. What was once a calm evening was now laden with a heavy tension.

Emerging from the woods, a spectral figure draped in white glided across the meadow. Her face, though pale and ethereal, bore an eternal sadness. Her gaze was downcast, avoiding the few lamplights dotting the park.

David's heart raced. He lifted his camera, but something inside warned him against it. There was an aura around this apparition, something deeply sorrowful, yet menacing.

His journalistic instincts overrode his fear. With a trembling hand, he took a photo. The flash lit up the surroundings, and for a split second, the White Lady stopped and looked straight at him. Her eyes were hollow, endless pools of black, and they bore into David's very soul.

He froze, the weight of her gaze pinning him to the bench. His breath caught, and the cold seemed to seep into his bones. The park, the world, faded away, and all that remained were those eyes.

Suddenly, he found himself in a different era. The park was unrecognizable, wilder, with dense woods. He stood before a grand manor, music and laughter echoing from within. Drawn to it, he approached the entrance.

Inside, a ball was in full swing. Men in tailcoats and women in flowing gowns danced across the room. David noticed her immediately. The woman in white, younger, vibrant, but with the same haunting eyes. She was in the arms of a dashing young man, their dance passionate, their gazes locked.

Whispers filled the air, tales of a forbidden love. She, Eleanor, the daughter of a wealthy baron, and he, Thomas, a stable boy. Their love, intense yet secret, was the scandal of Preston.

David watched as the night unfolded. The stolen glances, the fleeting touches. But as dawn approached, disaster struck. The baron, having learned of the secret trysts, flew into a rage. Thomas was dragged away, and Eleanor, in her white ballgown, was locked in the attic, her pleas echoing through the manor.

Days turned into weeks. The once vivacious Eleanor grew frail, her spirit breaking. One fateful night, unable to bear the separation, she flung herself from the attic window, her figure disappearing into the woods.

The vision shifted. David found himself back on the bench, the cold night air burning his lungs. The White Lady stood before him, her gaze filled with centuries of pain and longing.

"Why?" David croaked, his voice hoarse.

"I am bound," she whispered, her voice echoing with sorrow. "Bound to this land, searching for my love. But he is lost to me. And those who see me are drawn into my sorrow, forever."

David felt a pull, an irresistible urge to follow her, to join her in her endless search. His surroundings blurred, the ground beneath him seemed to shift and sway. He was being drawn into the abyss, into the eternal sadness of the White Lady.

Desperate, David reached into his pocket and pulled out the photo he had taken. With all his might, he tore it in half, breaking the connection. The White Lady let out an anguished scream, her form dissipating into the night.

Exhausted, David stumbled to his feet. The weight in the air had lifted, and the park was once again just a park. But the terror of that night, the haunting gaze of the White Lady, would remain with him forever.

He left Preston the next day, vowing never to return. The photo, or what remained of it, he locked away, a chilling reminder of the night he gazed upon the sorrowful spirit of Avenham Park.

And while the park remains a haven for many, when the sun sets, and the shadows grow long, a chilling melody can be heard, and a figure in white wanders the meadows, her heart forever yearning for a love lost to time.

CHAPTER 19:

The Drowned Souls of Canewdon Church

Canewdon, a quiet village nestled deep within the Essex countryside, held secrets darker than its most moonless nights. Its church, a formidable stone structure, stood tall amidst the rolling meadows, a beacon of faith for the devout. But the waters nearby, they whispered a different tale.

Caleb was a historian, a seeker of truths hidden within layers of time. The tale of Canewdon's drowned souls drew him to its grassy shores. Rumours said that souls lost at sea, those who met their doom in the tempestuous waters, still roamed the church grounds, searching for final redemption.

The night Caleb chose to visit was particularly eerie. Dark clouds swathed the moon, casting ghostly shadows across the landscape. A gentle fog curled up from the water, giving the world a surreal, dreamlike quality.

He reached the church just as the bells tolled midnight. The sound echoed, deep and foreboding, drowning out the distant lapping of the water. With each toll, the temperature seemed to drop, and the mist grew denser.

Shivering, Caleb approached the church doors. They groaned open at his touch, revealing the dim, candlelit interior. Rows of wooden pews led to a grand altar, behind which a vast stained-glass window depicted a shipwreck.

Caleb's gaze lingered on the window. In the ship's final moments, as its sails were swallowed by gargantuan waves, the faces of the doomed crew were etched in vivid colour. Their eyes, wide with terror, seemed almost lifelike.

As he studied the window, he heard it. A soft, mournful wail, like the cry of a lost child. Startled, Caleb turned, scanning the church. Nothing seemed out of place. Yet the cry persisted, growing louder, echoing throughout the church.

Suddenly, water began seeping through the church's stone walls. Puddles formed, growing rapidly, the water level rising with alarming speed. Caleb, panic rising, raced to the exit, but the doors wouldn't budge.

The water reached his knees, cold and unyielding. And then, emerging from the depths, figures began to take shape. Ethereal, translucent souls, their clothes tattered, their eyes hollow. They wailed in anguish, their cries echoing the ship's final moments.

Caleb recognized them. The faces from the stained-glass window, the crew of the doomed ship. They reached for him, their hands grasping, their expressions pleading. The weight of their sorrow, their eternal torment, pressed down on Caleb, threatening to drown him in a sea of despair.

Desperate, he lunged for the altar, hoping to find sanctuary. But as he reached it, a new figure emerged from the water. The captain, distinguishable by his grand hat and coat, his eyes filled with a haunting intensity. He approached Caleb, his voice deep and resonating, "You, landwalker, you bear witness to our curse. Every soul lost at sea near this sacred ground is bound here, unable to move on."

Caleb, gasping for breath, stammered, "How... how can I help?"

The captain's eyes bore into Caleb's soul. "You must find the one who cursed us. Settle the old score. Only then can we be free."

The water receded as quickly as it had risen, leaving Caleb drenched and shivering on the church floor. The ghostly apparitions vanished, but their desperate cries lingered in his ears.

Determined to help, Caleb began digging into the village's history. He discovered tales of a vengeful witch who, after being wronged by the ship's captain, had cursed the ship and its crew to eternal damnation.

Caleb's search led him to a grave, set apart from the rest, covered in creeping vines. The tombstone bore the witch's name, Elara. Legend said that Elara had once loved the captain. But in a fit of jealousy and rage, he had betrayed her, leading to her public shaming and eventual exile from the village. In her final moments, she had cast the curse, binding the ship's souls to the church grounds forever.

In the dead of night, under a sliver of a crescent moon, Caleb stood before Elara's grave. Armed with old rituals and incantations, he began to chant, hoping to appease the vengeful spirit.

The ground trembled, and a gust of wind tore through the cemetery. From the depths, Elara emerged, her form ethereal, her eyes burning with fury. "Why do you disturb my rest?" she hissed.

"I seek to free the souls you've bound," Caleb replied, voice trembling.

"Why should I? They wronged me. They deserve their fate!"

"They've suffered long enough. I beg you, release them."

Elara's gaze softened momentarily, memories of love and betrayal flashing in her eyes. After what felt like an eternity, she whispered, "Very well. But there's a price. One soul for many."

Before Caleb could react, the ground opened up beneath him, swallowing him whole.

The next morning, the villagers found the church grounds serene and peaceful, with no trace of the drowned souls. But nearby, fresh on Elara's grave, lay a new tombstone. Engraved upon it was Caleb's name, a testament to his sacrifice for the redemption of the damned.

In the years that followed, no soul ever reported seeing the drowned spirits of Canewdon Church. But on certain nights, when the moon was just a sliver and the wind whispered through the trees, one could hear the soft lament of a historian, forever bound to the land he sought to save.

CHAPTER 20:

The Haunting of the SS Great Britain

In the year 1843, the SS Great Britain was launched as a marvel of maritime engineering. A passenger ship so grand, it was said to be a beacon of British craftsmanship. But for all its architectural genius, the vessel held secrets as dark as the waters she sailed.

William Tremaine, a retired naval officer, had become an enthusiast of maritime lore. Following his early retirement due to a near-death experience at sea, he was often drawn to tales of ships and their voyages. The SS Great Britain, now anchored in Bristol, had a rich history with stories of opulent voyages, innovations, and adventures. However, there were whispered tales that after sundown, she transformed into a vessel of pure terror.

Intrigued, William decided to spend a night on board. He arrived at the dock just as the sun began to set, painting the sky with brilliant oranges and reds, contrasting the looming shadow of the ship. Armed with a lantern and a sense of rising anticipation, he stepped onto the vessel.

The ship, though silent, seemed to resonate with an energy of its own. The tales spoke of a luxurious first-class cabin that was said to be the heart of the hauntings. The lore spoke of Lady Elizabeth, a young bride traveling to

New York who mysteriously vanished during the voyage. Some say she never left the ship and that her spirit, tormented and trapped, roamed the very cabin she last occupied.

As William approached the first-class suites, the ship's timbers began to groan, as if protesting an unwelcome presence. The temperature plummeted, and the lantern's flame flickered erratically. A chilling breeze wafted through the corridors, carrying with it a faint aroma of vintage perfume. It was a scent William knew well; it was the same perfume his late wife used to wear.

Pushing the nostalgia aside, he reached Lady Elizabeth's suite. The door, aged and with paint chipped off, seemed to beckon him. Gathering courage, he pushed it open.

The room, bathed in silvery moonlight, appeared untouched by time. An ornate vanity, a sprawling bed, and a portrait of a young woman hung on the wall. As he stepped closer, the face in the portrait morphed, its features twisting into a mask of sheer terror. William's breath caught in his throat, and he felt an icy grip on his shoulder.

Whirling around, he came face to face with Lady Elizabeth. Her visage was pale, eyes hollow and bottomless, her wedding gown stained with saltwater and seaweed. She reached out, her touch cold as the deepest ocean.

"You shouldn't be here," she whispered, her voice echoing the sorrow of the abyss.

"I—I came to understand, to help," William stammered.

But before he could utter another word, the room began to change. Suddenly, he found himself in the midst of a raging storm. Titanic waves crashed against the ship, and the chilling winds howled with fury. And amidst the chaos, he saw her – Lady Elizabeth, standing at the ship's bow, facing the storm.

Terrified, William tried to reach her, but an invisible force held him back. As he watched in horror, a massive wave engulfed the ship, pulling Lady Elizabeth into its dark embrace.

The scene dissolved, and William found himself back in the room, drenched and gasping for breath. Lady Elizabeth, her form now less menacing, appeared beside him. Tears streamed down her face as she whispered, "It wasn't the sea that took me. It was despair."

She recounted the tale of her ill-fated voyage. Her husband, overwhelmed by gambling debts, had abandoned her mid-journey. Heartbroken and alone, she had chosen the depths over a life of disgrace.

Moved by her story, William felt a surge of determination. "You need peace, and I'll help you find it."

But Lady Elizabeth shook her head. "The ship is cursed, and so am I. Any soul that dares to unveil its secrets is bound to it forever."

A sinking feeling overcame William as the ship seemed to come alive. Walls groaned, floors creaked, and ghostly apparitions of past passengers appeared, their faces distorted in anguish.

In desperation, William raced towards the exit, but the ship was a labyrinth that twisted and turned on its own accord. As he ran, the drowned souls of the ship reached out, their fingers brushing against his skin, leaving burns in their wake.

Finally, he saw it - the exit. But as he neared it, the ground beneath him gave way, and he plunged into a watery abyss. The coldness enveloped him, and as he sank deeper, the weight of the ship's sorrow bore down on him.

The next morning, dock workers found the ship just as they had left it, silent and seemingly lifeless. But inside, in Lady Elizabeth's suite, they found William's lantern, still burning brightly.

Though his body was never found, mariners claim that on stormy nights, near the waters where the SS Great Britain once sailed, you can hear the cries of a man, intertwined with the lament of a heartbroken woman. A chilling reminder that some ships, no matter how grand, carry with them a cargo of unspeakable horror.

CHAPTER 21:

The Haunting of the Golden Fleece, York

There's a saying among the folk of York: "When dusk settles over the city, only the brave tread the cobblestones of the Shambles." It wasn't always this way, of course. In the heart of the ancient streets stood the Golden Fleece, a pub that had seen centuries pass its wooden beams, heard stories whispered over frothy ales, and held onto its own dark tales. The kind of tales that can make a grown man cry.

When Benjamin, an up-and-coming journalist, heard whispers about the inn being the most haunted in the entirety of York, he sensed a story. Intrigued, he booked a room and made his way there. For a man who didn't believe in the supernatural, this was merely a fun venture, an exploration. But he'd soon learn, the Golden Fleece wasn't a place for the faint-hearted.

The inn greeted him with its Tudor facade and low ceilings, exuding an old-world charm that immediately put him at ease. Eleanor, the barmaid with raven-black hair and bright blue eyes, handed him an iron key, its rust and age evident. "Room 4," she said, her voice a hushed whisper, "Just like you asked."

Night approached as Benjamin settled in. The room was quaint, with creaky floorboards and the light scent of aged wood. Deciding to start his research immediately, he made his way downstairs. The pub, filled with locals enjoying their evening drinks, held an atmosphere of laughter and joviality. A stark contrast to the tales he had heard.

Eleanor, noticing his curious glances, leaned in and whispered, "It's not the patrons you should fear, but the spirits that lurk after hours."

As hours passed and drinks flowed, Benjamin, feeling a light buzz, decided it was time to retire. Eleanor's words echoed in his ears, but he shrugged them off. After all, what harm could an old inn hold?

In the dead of night, a faint scratching began at the window. Groggily, Benjamin peered through the curtains, expecting to see a tree branch or perhaps a stray bird. Instead, his eyes met with those of a woman outside, her pale face pressed against the glass, her eyes empty sockets. Stifling a scream, he stumbled back. When he dared to look again, she was gone.

Cold sweat covered his brow. He told himself it was a dream, a result of too much alcohol. But as he tried to drift off to sleep again, the floorboards creaked. Footsteps approached, each step heavier than the last. Benjamin's heart raced. The door handle began to turn, and slowly, it creaked open.

In the dim moonlight, he saw her - the same woman, her long white dress flowing, her face a mask of sorrow and rage. Her empty eyes locked onto his, and Benjamin felt a cold grip on his soul.

"Why?" she whispered, her voice echoing the pain of centuries. "Why did they do it?"

Frozen in terror, Benjamin couldn't reply. She approached, her form flickering like a candle's flame, her fingers reaching out to touch his face. They felt icy cold, like the depths of winter.

Tales of Lady Peckett, the wife of a former mayor and resident of the inn, rushed back to him. Legends spoke of her wandering the inn, searching for her husband who had betrayed her. She had taken her own life in this very room.

In a desperate bid to escape, Benjamin lunged for the door. But the corridor outside held its own horrors. Ghostly soldiers from a time long past marched in formation, their vacant stares piercing the darkness. Their murmurs of battles and death filled the air.

Panic took hold as Benjamin rushed downstairs. But the pub was no longer the haven it was earlier. Shadows danced on the walls, and ghostly patrons sat with empty mugs, their hollow laughter chilling him to the bone.

At the bar, Eleanor stood, her appearance now ghastly, her bright blue eyes replaced by voids of endless darkness. "I did warn you," she whispered, her voice now a grotesque parody of her earlier self.

Desperate, Benjamin sprinted for the exit. But every door he opened led him back to the same room – Room 4.

Lady Peckett awaited each time, her sorrow-filled eyes pleading, her ghostly fingers reaching out to him.

The night seemed endless, a maze of horrors from which there was no escape. As dawn approached, Benjamin, now a mere shadow of his former self, found himself back in the room, Lady Peckett's chilling presence ever constant.

When the morning staff entered the inn, they found Room 4 empty. The bed was untouched, the window slightly open. But on the desk lay Benjamin's notebook. It was filled with frenzied writings, detailing every horror he had witnessed. The last entry was a simple sentence, written with a shaky hand: "She is still here."

From that day on, patrons whispered of the journalist who came seeking a story and became one himself. The Golden Fleece, with its dark history and restless spirits, stood as a chilling reminder that some tales are best left untold. For in the heart of York, there's a room that holds a story, a room where the boundary between the living and the dead is terrifyingly thin.

CHAPTER 22:

The Ghost of Anne Bronte at Scarborough

Scarborough. A coastal town in North Yorkshire, known for its spa town history, its medieval castle, and a particular ghost story that keeps tourists awake at night.

Marcus was a retired literature professor. Spending most of his life surrounded by books, he had developed a particular fascination with the Bronte sisters. Charlotte and Emily always took centre stage in discussions, their novels analysed and reanalysed. But Anne? She was the quiet sister, her voice barely heard, overshadowed by the success of her siblings.

In his search for forgotten literary tales, Marcus decided to visit Scarborough, where Anne Bronte was buried. He had heard whispers of her restless spirit, of mournful apparitions near her gravesite. He wanted to see for himself, to maybe catch a glimpse of the ghost of Anne Bronte.

He rented a cottage overlooking the sea, just a short walk from St Mary's churchyard where Anne was laid to rest. On his first evening in Scarborough, Marcus ventured to the graveyard. It was still light outside, the sun setting in the horizon, casting the old gravestones in soft, golden hues.

As he approached Anne's grave, he felt a sudden drop in temperature. The gentle breeze that had been accompanying him now felt like cold fingers grazing his skin. He reached the grave – a simple stone reading 'Here lie the remains of Anne Bronte'. Standing there, he felt an overwhelming sense of sadness, the weight of a life overshadowed, of a voice stifled.

Night began to fall. Marcus turned to leave when he heard a faint sound. A woman's voice, singing a mournful tune. He looked around, trying to locate the source, but there was no one in sight. The voice seemed to be coming from the sea, the waves crashing in harmony with the sorrowful melody.

Curiosity piqued, Marcus decided to visit the local pub, hoping to gather some tales about Anne's ghostly presence. The locals, huddled in groups, eyed him warily as he entered. Sitting at the bar, he ordered a drink and struck up a conversation with the bartender.

"Ah, Anne Bronte," the bartender sighed, his face turning a shade paler. "She never really left, you know? They say she wanders the beach at night, her spirit restless, searching for something. Or someone."

Marcus's interest was piqued. "Has anyone seen her?"

The bartender looked around, making sure no one was eavesdropping. "There's a tale of a man, a writer like yourself. He came here years ago, hoping to see Anne. And see her he did. On a stormy night, he was walking along the beach when he spotted a woman in a long white dress, her face hidden by a veil. She was singing that same mournful tune. He approached her, called out to her, but she vanished into thin air."

The story sent shivers down Marcus's spine. But he was not one to be deterred. The following night, he decided to take a midnight stroll along the beach.

The moon cast a silvery glow on the sands, the waves crashing loudly. As he walked, the cold wind picked up, whipping his face. And then he heard it. The same song he had heard at the graveyard. It grew louder, more pronounced. He followed the sound until he saw her.

A woman in a white dress, her back turned to him. The wind seemed to dance around her, but the dress remained still. Marcus approached cautiously, the sands beneath his feet muffling his steps.

"Anne?" he called out softly.

The figure paused, her singing stopping abruptly. Slowly, she turned to face him. Her face was hidden beneath a thick veil, but her eyes... They were pools of profound sadness, staring deep into his soul.

"Why are you here?" she whispered, her voice echoing the pain of a lifetime.

"I wanted to see you," Marcus replied, his voice trembling. "To hear your story."

She stared at him for what felt like an eternity. Then, lifting her veil, she revealed her face. Pale, almost translucent, with deep-set eyes that had seen too much pain.

"They forgot me," she said, tears streaming down her face. "I was always in their shadows, my voice never heard. Even in death, I remain forgotten."

Marcus, moved by her pain, reached out to touch her. But his fingers passed right through her, sending a jolt of cold through his body.

"You can't help me," she whispered, her voice filled with despair. "No one can."

And with that, she vanished, leaving Marcus alone on the beach, the weight of her sorrow pressing down on him.

He returned to his cottage, a heavy heart inside his chest. Sleep eluded him, images of the ghostly Anne haunting his dreams. The next morning, he found himself at her grave, laying down a bouquet of white roses.

The townsfolk whispered among themselves, watching the outsider paying his respects to their forgotten ghost. And as Marcus left Scarborough, he carried with him the tale of Anne Bronte, ensuring that her voice, though ghostly, would never be silenced again.

But the beach... the beach remained haunted. To this day, on stormy nights, if you listen closely, you can hear the mournful tune of Anne Bronte, singing her tale of woe, her spirit forever restless, forever searching.

CHAPTER 23:

The Phantom Highwayman of Dartmoor

The rugged landscape of Dartmoor, with its wild, windswept moors and towering tors, was a place of natural beauty and ancient mysteries. For centuries, stories of supernatural beings and ghostly apparitions had been whispered amongst the locals. But none were as chilling or as widely recounted as the tale of the Phantom Highwayman.

Anna, a London-based journalist, was dispatched to Dartmoor to cover a piece on the UK's most haunted places. She had been briefed on the local legends, but none intrigued her as much as the spectral highwayman, known to appear on foggy nights, seeking out lone travellers.

Anna's base was a quaint inn, The Tor's Rest, nestled in a small village at the edge of the moor. Upon her arrival, she was greeted warmly by the innkeeper, a stout man named George. As the evening wore on and the patrons began to share stories over drinks, Anna's curiosity about the phantom grew. She decided to pose the question directly.

"Tell me about the Highwayman of Dartmoor," Anna inquired.

A hush fell over the inn's common room. George hesitated, then began in a hushed tone, "They say he was a cruel man when he was alive, robbing and sometimes killing travellers. His reign of terror ended when the locals banded together and ambushed him one night. They say he was left to die on the moor, but his spirit never moved on."

A weathered old man from the corner, known as Old Tom, piped up, "He's real, that one. Seen him myself, on a foggy night years ago. Eyes glowing like coals, they were. He rides a pitch-black steed, and when he catches you, your soul is his."

Anna shivered but wasn't convinced. "Surely it's just a story," she chuckled.

George looked her dead in the eye. "There have been disappearances, Miss. Lone travellers on the moor, gone without a trace. Only their abandoned vehicles left behind."

Feeling a mixture of scepticism and intrigue, Anna decided she'd venture onto the moor the following evening. If there was a story to be had, she was determined to uncover it.

The next day was dreary. Thick fog enveloped Dartmoor, reducing visibility to mere meters. By evening, Anna, armed with her camera and recorder, set out. She had been walking for hours with no sign of anything unusual. Just as she was about to give up, a distant sound reached her ears – the echoing clatter of hooves on the stony path.

Straining her eyes, she saw a shadowy figure on horseback emerging from the fog. The horse was dark, its eyes red and piercing. Atop it sat a man, his face obscured by a wide-brimmed hat, a long cloak billowing behind him. Anna's heart raced as she hid behind a large boulder, camera at the ready.

The highwayman paused, sniffing the air like a predator. "Who dares tread on my moor?" he boomed, his voice echoing eerily. Without waiting, he spurred his horse forward, charging into the fog.

Anna took a deep breath, feeling both fear and excitement. She decided to follow him, keeping a safe distance. But the moor was disorienting in the fog, and she soon realized she was hopelessly lost. Panic set in as the temperature dropped and the fog grew denser.

Suddenly, the clatter of hooves sounded again, closer this time. Anna turned to see the highwayman charging directly at her. She tried to run, but her feet felt glued to the spot. The last thing she saw before everything went black was the highwayman's glowing eyes.

Anna awoke to find herself in an ancient stone circle, the highwayman standing over her. "Why have you come here?" he hissed.

Anna stammered, "I... I wanted to know your story."

The highwayman laughed, a sound devoid of mirth. "You city folk, always seeking stories. I was betrayed, left to die on this very moor. Now, I roam, taking what was taken from me."

Anna, gathering courage, retorted, "But those people you took, they had nothing to do with your death!"

The highwayman leaned in, his face inches from hers. "Every soul I take is a step closer to my release from this torment. And now, you're here."

Anna felt an icy grip on her heart. "You can't have my soul," she whispered defiantly.

The phantom chuckled. "You came to my domain, seeking a story. Well, here it is." With that, he lunged at her.

Suddenly, a bright light pierced the fog. The highwayman recoiled, shielding his eyes. From the light emerged Old Tom, holding aloft a lantern. "Be gone, vile spirit!" he shouted.

The highwayman hissed, disappearing into the fog. Tom rushed to Anna's side, helping her to her feet. "You shouldn't have come here alone, lass," he said.

Anna, still in shock, nodded. "I was foolish. Thank you."

Tom guided Anna back to the village, the lantern's light warding off the encroaching darkness. Anna soon left Dartmoor, her story incomplete, but with a newfound respect for legends.

The Phantom Highwayman still roams Dartmoor, seeking souls to quench his insatiable thirst. Those who know the legend steer clear of the moor on foggy nights, lest they become another chapter in the terrifying tale of the Phantom Highwayman of Dartmoor.

CHAPTER 24:

The Ghost of Greyfriars Bobby, Edinburgh

Edinburgh, with its ancient buildings and rich history, had seen its share of tragedies. But sometimes, tales of loyalty surpassed even the saddest of human stories, reaching deep into the realm of the supernatural.

Rachel was an avid dog lover. When she heard about Greyfriars Bobby, the loyal Skye terrier who stood guard over his owner's grave for 14 years, she was deeply touched. She decided to visit Edinburgh, specifically to see the famed Greyfriars Kirkyard.

Staying at a B&B close to the graveyard, Rachel planned her visit. She had heard the stories, of course – tales of people spotting a small, shadowy canine figure near a certain grave, even feeling a cold, wet nose nudging their hand in the chill of the night. But Rachel was a sceptic. She believed Bobby's story was touching but saw the ghost tales as mere urban legend.

The first day, she took a guided tour of the Kirkyard, listening to the guide recount Bobby's tale amidst others of betrayal, plague, and witch hunts. The graveyard was steeped in history, every corner hiding a story, every stone whispering secrets of the past.

Nightfall in Edinburgh was swift, the city's street lights casting eerie, long shadows. Driven by a mix of curiosity and bravado, Rachel decided to visit the Kirkyard again, alone. She wanted a moment with Bobby's statue without the tourist crowd.

The iron gates of the Kirkyard creaked as she pushed them open. The silvery moonlight illuminated the graves, creating an ethereal atmosphere. Rachel felt an odd mix of calm and trepidation.

Walking toward Bobby's statue, she felt a sudden drop in temperature. She wrapped her jacket tighter around her, attributing it to the general chill of Scottish nights. However, as she neared the statue, she heard a soft whimper.

Startled, Rachel looked around, trying to locate the source. There, near a grave, sat a small dog, its silhouette barely discernible in the dim light. Rachel approached cautiously. "Hey there," she whispered, extending a hand. The dog looked up, its eyes reflecting a deep sadness.

Suddenly, a gust of wind blew, and Rachel felt a chill run down her spine. The dog had vanished.

Shaken, she decided it was best to leave. As she retraced her steps, she felt a soft tugging at her jeans. Looking down, she saw nothing, but the sensation was unmistakable – like a small dog nipping playfully.

Heart pounding, Rachel hurried towards the gate. She could hear soft, echoing barks, growing increasingly desperate and mournful. The wind seemed to carry whispers, "Stay... don't leave..."

As she reached the gate, a deep, guttural growl rumbled from behind. Rachel dared not look back. She fumbled with the latch, her fingers numb with cold and fear. The growling grew louder, closer. The air was thick with tension.

With a final push, Rachel burst through the gates, stumbling onto the pavement outside. Gasping for breath, she looked back at the graveyard. It seemed calm, the moonlight casting a peaceful glow.

But Rachel knew better. She had felt the profound sorrow, the yearning. She realized the tales weren't just urban legends. The spirit of Bobby was real, forever bound to the place of his loyalty, forever searching for companionship, forever restless.

She returned to her B&B, deeply unsettled. Sleep eluded her. Every little noise, every creak of the old building, sent her heart racing.

The next morning, Rachel decided to visit the Kirkyard one last time. Daylight brought a different perspective, but the memories of the previous night were still fresh. She approached the statue of Bobby, laying a bouquet of flowers at its base.

As she turned to leave, she felt a cold, wet sensation on her hand. Looking down, there was no dog in sight. However, the unmistakable feel of a dog's lick lingered.

That was Rachel's last visit to Greyfriars Kirkyard. She left Edinburgh with a heavy heart, the tale of Bobby's loyalty taking on a deeper, more haunting meaning. She realized some bonds, even in death, were too strong to break. And sometimes, loyalty could become an eternal prison, trapping souls in a relentless cycle of hope, yearning, and sorrow.

Years later, Rachel would recount her experience to those willing to listen. Many dismissed it as mere imagination, the effects of the eerie ambiance of an old graveyard at night. But Rachel knew what she had felt. The story of Greyfriars Bobby wasn't just a tale of undying loyalty; it was a chilling reminder of the chains that bind us, even beyond the grave.

CHAPTER 25:

Dorothy Southworth of Samlesbury Hall, Lancashire

The ancient stone walls of Samlesbury Hall had been privy to countless secrets, tales of love, betrayals, and a sinister darkness lurking in its corners. Built in 1325, this sprawling mansion had seen its share of residents, guests, and passersby. But the hall's eeriest tale wasn't one of its majestic architecture or its vintage tapestries. It was the story of Dorothy Southworth, a young woman accused of witchcraft in 1612.

Clara, an investigative journalist with a penchant for all things supernatural, found herself drawn to Samlesbury Hall. She'd heard whispers of Dorothy's spirit, a tormented soul eternally trapped within the confines of the hall. The very mention of Dorothy's name sent shivers down the spines of the local folk. Many claimed to have seen her apparition, a dark figure, wandering the hallways, the gardens, and especially near the old chapel.

With her trusty notebook and camera, Clara decided to spend a night in Samlesbury Hall. The place was now a heritage site and was open to visitors, with parts of it renovated into a boutique hotel. The receptionist, a petite woman with silver hair, handed Clara the keys to her room but warned, "Stay away from the chapel after dark, dear."

Clara chuckled, thinking it to be a marketing gimmick. "Is that where Dorothy roams?" she teased.

The receptionist's face turned ashen. "I've worked here for thirty years," she whispered. "And there's something about that chapel. People hear chants, crying... some even claim to see her. Just... stay away."

Clara nodded but wasn't one to be easily deterred. After settling in, she began exploring. The vast corridors, grand rooms, and medieval architecture were captivating. But as evening approached, she felt an inexplicable draw to the chapel.

Outside, the sun cast a deep orange glow, the horizon tinged with hues of purple and pink. The chapel, with its gothic windows and moss-covered stones, looked serene. Pushing open the heavy wooden door, Clara stepped inside.

The chapel was cool and dark, the fading sunlight casting eerie patterns on the floor. In the distance, Clara could hear the soft rustle of leaves, the chirping of birds. But as she ventured further in, a palpable silence enveloped her.

She felt it before she saw it. A sudden drop in temperature, a feeling of being watched. Turning around, she was met with an ethereal sight. There, near the altar, stood a figure draped in a dark robe, her face obscured by shadows. The air around her seemed to shimmer, her form wavering like a mirage.

Frozen in place, Clara could only watch as the figure began to glide towards her. Her instincts screamed at her to run, but her feet felt glued to the spot. As the figure drew closer, Clara could make out a face, young and beautiful, but with eyes that mirrored centuries of pain.

"Dorothy?" Clara whispered.

The figure stopped, tilting her head, her gaze piercing through Clara. Then, in a voice that sounded like a mix of a sigh and a cry, she spoke, "They accused me, tortured me, claimed I consorted with the devil. All for love..."

Clara, still rooted to the spot, managed to ask, "Love?"

Dorothy's form seemed to solidify, the shimmering reducing. "I loved a man they disapproved of. They called our love a sin, a pact with the devil. They took him from me, and then they came for me."

The sadness in her voice was palpable. But before Clara could respond, she felt a sharp gust of wind. Papers flew, candles flickered, and the entire chapel seemed to come alive with a cacophony of voices. Chants, cries, screams – it was as if the walls were replaying the tragic events of the past.

Clara felt herself being lifted off the ground, the force pushing her towards the chapel's exit. As she stumbled out, gasping for breath, the door slammed shut behind her.

The night was now inky dark, the moon casting a pale light over the grounds. Clara, heart pounding, made her way back to the main building. The receptionist was waiting, her face a mix of concern and "I told you so."

"You saw her, didn't you?" she asked.

Clara nodded, still trying to process what had transpired.

"That chapel," the receptionist whispered, "is where they held her trial, declared her a witch, and then... hung her. They say her spirit never left, forever searching for her lost love."

Clara spent a restless night, the sounds of the chapel replaying in her mind. By dawn, she was packed and ready to leave. Samlesbury Hall, with its dark history, was too much even for an avid supernatural enthusiast like her.

As she drove away, she could've sworn she saw a figure in the rearview mirror, standing near the chapel, her form shimmering in the morning light. The face was obscured, but the eyes – those haunting eyes – seemed to be pleading, begging for release from an eternal prison of pain.

Clara never returned to Samlesbury Hall. But the story of Dorothy Southworth, a tale of love, betrayal, and a cursed existence, stayed with her. Some places, Clara realized, held onto their past so tightly that the lines between the living and the dead blurred, trapping souls in an endless loop of torment.

CHAPTER 26:

The Mackenzie Poltergeist, Greyfriars Kirkyard, Edinburgh

The rains came down hard on the streets of Edinburgh, with each drop splattering on the ancient cobblestones, echoing history's many secrets. Tourists, though fond of the city's rich past, often overlooked a small, less popular section of the town - the Greyfriars Kirkyard. The history it harboured wasn't for the faint of heart. The tomb of George Mackenzie lay here, a site that had witnessed countless inexplicable injuries and horror tales.

Camille, an American grad student with a fervent curiosity in Scottish paranormal history, had travelled across the pond to delve into the Kirkyard's mysteries. She was warned, advised, and even ridiculed for her intentions. But a burning quest for truth propelled her steps, right into the heart of the cemetery one fateful evening.

As she entered the graveyard, Camille felt an instant drop in temperature, an eerie coldness that was oddly isolated from the outside climate. The ancient tombstones, chiselled with the grief of centuries, stood as silent witnesses, their shadows morphing and distorting with the setting sun.

The Black Mausoleum, the resting place of George Mackenzie, was Camille's primary destination. Mackenzie, known in his time as "Bloody Mackenzie," was a lawyer responsible for the deaths of numerous Covenanters, held in a field prison just beside the Kirkyard. His malevolent spirit was believed to be restless, causing disturbances for centuries after his death.

The tales told of visitors leaving the Kirkyard with scratches, burns, bruises, and even broken bones. Others spoke of sudden feelings of nausea, dizziness, or overwhelming dread. But Camille, armed with her voice recorder and camera, was undeterred. She approached the tomb, noting the air's pungency, a rotting scent mixed with a metallic twang, like old blood.

As she neared the Black Mausoleum, she felt an invisible wall of cold air, a palpable force pushing her away. Every logical bone in her body screamed to leave, but Camille pressed on.

"George Mackenzie, if you're here, give me a sign," she whispered, her voice echoing more than it should've in the open space. But the graveyard remained silent, save for the distant patter of rain and the wind's whispers.

Determined, she continued. "I want to know your story, George. The true story. Why do you harm the living?"

She waited, her breath visible in the cold. Just when she was about to dismiss her efforts, a violent gust of wind howled through the Mausoleum, extinguishing her torchlight. In the dark, Camille felt the ground shift beneath her. Panic surged through her veins.

From the depths of the darkness, a voice rasped, echoing the cruelty of centuries, "Why? Because they dare to disturb. Because the pain I gave others in life carries on in death."

Her torchlight flickered back to life, revealing the shadowy figure of a man dressed in 17th-century garb, his face pale and eyes hollow, an eternal smirk carved onto his lips.

Camille stumbled back, her heart hammering. "What do you want?"

"The torment of the living," Mackenzie's spectre replied. "They imprisoned and killed my brethren, and I imprisoned and killed theirs. But in death, my power grows, reaching beyond the confines of this tomb."

Camille tried to retreat, but her legs felt glued to the spot. "Why tell me this?"

The ghost smirked. "Because, dear Camille, you sought the truth. Now you have it. You've seen the face of the Mackenzie Poltergeist. And those who see, never forget."

Suddenly, the weight around Camille's legs vanished, and she fled, not looking back, driven by primal fear. The winding pathways seemed to shift and change, gravestones looming like monstrous spectres, guiding or perhaps mocking her desperate escape. Her breath came out in ragged gasps, the cold air burning her lungs.

It was only when she hit the main streets of Edinburgh, with its welcoming lights and the murmurs of nightlife, did she dare to stop, collapsing against a wall, heart racing.

She might've dismissed the entire encounter as a figment of her overactive imagination if not for one thing. Later that night, as she undressed in her hotel room, she noticed them – numerous fresh, red scratches running down her back. They weren't random but seemed to spell out a word: "Remember."

And Camille did. The trauma of that night haunted her dreams for the rest of her days. The world branded her another victim of the Mackenzie Poltergeist's malevolence. She never returned to Edinburgh, but she didn't need to. For the true horror wasn't just in the Kirkyard or the tomb. It was in the knowledge that some evils, once confronted, never truly let go.

The Mackenzie Poltergeist was more than just an old ghost story. It was a testament to the enduring power of hatred and cruelty, a warning that some spirits were better left undisturbed. And as for Camille, she learned the hardest truth of all – that seeking darkness might just mean the darkness starts seeking you back.

CHAPTER 27:

The Ghosts of Kenilworth Castle, Warwickshire

The town of Kenilworth, with its rich tapestry of history, had always been a hotspot for tourists. At the heart of it was the Kenilworth Castle, a sprawling ruin with turrets that cut jagged lines against the sky. For all its grandeur, locals knew better than to tread near it after dark.

Martin Thorne had recently moved to Kenilworth for work. As an aspiring novelist, he thought the historical setting would provide ample inspiration. His rented cottage was just a short walk away from the castle. The place was picturesque in the day, with kids running around, and families having picnics. But come nightfall, the castle had a different aura, one that most residents of Kenilworth respected, if not feared.

One evening, as Martin struggled with writer's block, a knock on his door jolted him from his trance. It was his elderly neighbour, Mrs. Whittle.

"Evening, Martin," she said, her voice like old paper. "I noticed your lights on. Still up writing your stories?"

"Yes," he replied, rubbing his temples. "But not getting very far, to be honest."

Mrs. Whittle leaned in closer, her pale blue eyes twinkling with mischief. "If it's a story you're looking for, have you thought about the castle?"

Martin raised an eyebrow. "What about it?"

She beckoned him to sit, and as he did, she began her tale.

Years ago, Kenilworth Castle wasn't just a tourist attraction. It was a place of grandeur, of parties and feasts. Among its most frequent guests was Lady Eleanor. Beautiful and headstrong, Eleanor was the talk of the town, not just for her beauty but for her romances. It was said that she had affairs with many men, some of them even meeting tragic ends. But her most scandalous affair was with a young footman named Thomas.

Their secret trysts in the hidden corners of the castle became the stuff of legends. But, like all secrets, it wasn't long before they were discovered. The scandal was too much. Eleanor was confined to the castle, and Thomas was never seen again. Heartbroken, Eleanor was said to have flung herself from the highest turret, her despairing wail echoing throughout the castle.

Martin listened, captivated. When Mrs. Whittle finished, he asked, "So you believe the castle is haunted by Eleanor?"

Mrs. Whittle nodded. "Not just by her. There are others too. The men she was involved with, and of course, poor Thomas. They say he still roams the castle, looking for his lost love."

That night, Martin couldn't sleep. The story stirred something in him. Armed with a torch, he decided to explore the castle. If he could feel the history, maybe the words would flow.

The night was unusually cold, the moon a mere crescent. As Martin approached the castle, its massive silhouette seemed to loom and shift. The wind carried whispers, unintelligible but eerily rhythmic. He shook off the uneasy feeling and entered.

Inside, the ruins took on a different character. The walls seemed to breathe, and shadows flickered like old memories trying to resurface. Martin felt a chill, deeper than the cold air, as he ventured deeper.

Suddenly, a faint cry echoed. It was a woman's voice, filled with anguish. Martin's heart raced, but he pressed on, drawn by the sound. He reached the chamber where Eleanor was said to have been confined. The room was cold, the air thick with despair. On the floor was an old pendant, tarnished but still showing a beautiful portrait of a woman, undoubtedly Eleanor.

Martin heard footsteps, light but deliberate. Turning around, he came face to face with a spectral figure – Lady Eleanor. Her once-beautiful visage marred by tears and anguish. Behind her, more phantoms appeared, each representing her past lovers, their faces contorted in pain and betrayal.

But the most tragic of them all was the apparition of Thomas, his face pale and his eyes filled with an eternal yearning. He reached out to Eleanor, but she, consumed by her guilt and sorrow, drew away.

The phantoms advanced toward Martin, their intentions unclear. Fear gripped him as he felt the weight of their collective tragedies. It was then that he realized he wasn't just a witness; he was part of their story now. Eleanor's ghostly hand reached out, her fingers mere inches from his face.

Suddenly, a loud bell tolled. The first light of dawn began to seep through. The spirits began to fade, their lamentations growing fainter. Martin, panting and drenched in sweat, rushed out of the castle.

The next morning, he packed his bags. The tale had given him enough material for a lifetime, but he knew he couldn't stay another night near the castle. As he drove away, he glanced at the rearview mirror, half-expecting to see Eleanor's sorrowful eyes. But there was nothing.

The castle resumed its daytime demeanour, serene and majestic. But those who know its secrets, like Mrs. Whittle and now Martin, would always feel the weight of the tragic tales it held within its walls. And they would always remember that in the heart of Kenilworth, when darkness falls, the past comes alive, seeking solace and, perhaps, a new story to tell.

CHAPTER 28:

The Chillingham Castle Ghosts, Northumberland

Elliot had never believed in ghost stories. He found them fascinating, yes, but in a "thank God that's not real" kind of way. So, when his girlfriend, Clara, booked them a weekend at Chillingham Castle, he took it as an exciting getaway rather than a venture into the supernatural.

Chillingham Castle stood proudly, its stone walls seeming to whisper of age-old secrets. On their first evening, the couple went for a walk around the castle grounds. They passed by ancient trees and small footbridges crossing over tranquil ponds. All was peaceful, except for the quiet rustle of leaves and the occasional chirp of a cricket.

After a while, Clara grabbed a brochure detailing the castle's history from a stand nearby. As she read aloud, Elliot's scepticism was met with a subtle unease. The castle was notorious for its tales of haunting, most notably by John Sage, a torturer during the castle's dark history, and the Radiant Boy, a young child who would appear in one of the castle's rooms, his cries echoing through the night.

That night, they stayed in a room known for its paranormal activities but seemed ordinary. A four-poster bed, with velvet curtains and a heavy oak door. Yet, there was something undeniably eerie about the dim candlelight casting flickering shadows on the stone walls.

Clara, ever the believer, set up a recorder, hoping to catch some ghostly voices. Elliot chuckled at the setup but indulged her. They decided to explore the castle at midnight.

As the grandfather clock downstairs struck twelve, they began their journey. Moving from room to room, they marvelled at the ancient artifacts and portraits of stern-looking nobles.

Suddenly, Clara froze. She motioned for Elliot to be silent. A faint cry echoed through the corridor. Following the sound, they arrived at a room where the cry grew louder, more desperate. The Blue Boy's room.

They slowly pushed the door open. Nothing. The room was cold, much colder than the others, but empty. They were about to leave when Clara's recorder buzzed to life on its own. A young voice echoed, "Help me..."

Clara and Elliot exchanged terrified glances. Wanting to find the source, they moved deeper into the castle. As they navigated through the narrow, winding corridors, a chilling breeze met them. It was unnatural, almost sentient, and it guided them toward the castle's dungeons.

Here, the weight of history pressed upon them. Chains hung from the walls, and instruments of torture lay forgotten in the corners. But one thing stood out - a wooden rack in the middle of the room. Suddenly, the wind howled, and the torches lining the room went out. In the pitch black, they heard the heavy breathing of someone else. Or something.

Terrified, they tried to retrace their steps, but every turn led them deeper into the labyrinthine dungeon. They felt an oppressive presence, a rage that permeated the very stones of the castle.

Suddenly, the faint glimmer of torchlight illuminated a figure ahead. It was a man, ancient and haggard, with scars crisscrossing his face. It was John Sage. His eyes, devoid of any humanity, fixed on the couple, and with a sinister smile, he began moving towards them.

As Sage approached, the spirits of his past victims materialized around him. Men, women, children, their faces twisted in anguish, joined in the pursuit. Elliot grabbed Clara's hand, pulling her as they desperately sought an escape. They stumbled upon a narrow staircase leading upwards.

Climbing the steps two at a time, they burst into the open air of the castle courtyard. The ghosts were gone. Taking a moment to catch their breath, they hurried back to their room, barricading the door.

The night was restless. Every shadow seemed to hide a spectre, every gust of wind carried tortured cries. But dawn eventually broke, and with it, the weight of the night lifted.

The next morning, they checked out, vowing never to return. As they left, the innkeeper handed them the recorder Clara had forgotten in the room. On the journey home, curiosity got the better of them. They pressed play.

The voice of John Sage echoed, "You can leave the castle, but the castle will never leave you."

For weeks after, Elliot and Clara were plagued by nightmares. The cries of the Radiant Boy echoed in their sleep, and they would often wake up, feeling the icy grip of phantom hands around their ankles.

They soon realized the castle's curse was real. One fateful night, Elliot awoke to find Clara gone. Searching the house, he found her outside, standing still, looking into the distance. Following her gaze, he saw the familiar silhouette of Chillingham Castle, bathed in moonlight, looming over them, even though they were miles away.

Clara turned to him, her eyes vacant. In a voice not her own, she whispered, "The castle calls us back."

And with that, the ground beneath them gave way, swallowing them into the darkness, leaving nothing but the echo of the Radiant Boy's cries. The castle had claimed two more souls, forever binding them to its haunting legacy.

CHAPTER 29:

The Ghosts of Bodmin Moor, Cornwall

The moors, especially the desolate and expansive ones like Bodmin, are places that easily capture the imagination. When the dense fog rolls in, as it often does, the landscape becomes an alien world, devoid of sound save for the lonely whistle of the wind.

Jenny, a photographer with a penchant for landscapes and old legends, had arrived at Bodmin in search of Charlotte Dymond's ghost. The story of Charlotte was as tragic as they come—a young girl, full of life and dreams, murdered in cold blood in 1844. The lore said that on foggy nights, one might see Charlotte wandering the moors, her white dress stained with the muddy scars of the earth and the crimson reminder of her untimely demise.

Jenny set up camp near the footpath, which was popular among hikers. As night approached, a dense blanket of fog enveloped the area. It was the perfect setting for capturing the eerie beauty of Bodmin. She could barely see beyond a few feet, the fog consuming everything, including the sounds. It was as if the world beyond had ceased to exist.

Switching on her torchlight, she began her venture deep into the moor, camera at the ready. Every now and then, she would stop to take a shot—the hauntingly beautiful expanse of the moor, the silhouette of a lone tree, or the subtle play of the torchlight against the thick mist.

As she wandered further from her camp, the fog grew thicker, and she felt an unmistakable sensation of being watched. She chalked it up to the solitude and the creepy tales associated with Bodmin. A rustle to her left made her pause. Probably an animal, she thought, but she aimed her torchlight in that direction regardless.

A blood-curdling scream tore through the silence, echoing all around her. Jenny's heart raced, the beam of her torch wavering as she frantically scanned the surroundings. Just as suddenly, the scream faded, and the oppressive silence returned.

She began to retrace her steps, her initial enthusiasm replaced with growing unease. The fog, instead of lifting, seemed to grow denser, distorting her sense of direction. Every tree, every rock seemed to morph into ominous figures, only to dissipate when she shined her torch upon them.

Jenny's heart pounded as she remembered the tale of Charlotte. Murdered by her lover, her body dumped unceremoniously, she was said to haunt these moors, seeking justice or perhaps simply yearning for the life that was stolen from her.

It was then that Jenny saw her—a spectral figure in a white dress, stained with dark patches, standing a few feet away. The woman's face was pale, her eyes hollow, with dark rivulets running down her cheeks, reminiscent of tear tracks.

"Charlotte?" Jenny whispered, frozen in place.

The figure didn't respond but slowly began to move towards Jenny, her feet hovering just above the ground, her gaze fixed intently on the living intruder. A cold wind picked up, swirling around Jenny, and she felt an overwhelming sadness, so palpable that it threatened to crush her.

Unable to bear it, Jenny turned and ran, the fog seemingly parting to guide her away from the apparition. Her breath came in ragged gasps, her lungs burning from the cold air. The haunting visage of Charlotte, however, was etched into her mind.

She stumbled upon her camp, collapsing near her tent, the cold ground a welcome sensation against her heated skin. Taking a moment to catch her breath, she glanced around, half-expecting Charlotte to emerge from the mist.

But the night was quiet, save for the distant hoot of an owl. The fog had lifted slightly, and the moonlight filtered through, casting an ethereal glow on the moor.

Jenny packed up her gear and made her way back to her car. As she drove away, she took one last look at the vast expanse of Bodmin Moor. And there, standing a distance away, was the ethereal figure of Charlotte, watching her, a silent guardian of the moors.

Jenny's photographs from that night were like no other. The desolate beauty of Bodmin Moor, accentuated by the mist and moonlight, was captured in all its haunting splendour. But one photograph stood out. It showed a vague outline of a woman in a white dress, standing amidst the fog. The image was slightly blurred, but the pain, the sorrow in those eyes, was unmistakable.

Jenny never returned to Bodmin. She had come looking for a ghost story and had found it. But more than fear, she felt an overwhelming sadness for Charlotte. A life cut short, a spirit forever wandering the moors, looking for solace, for justice.

The photograph of Charlotte took pride of place in Jenny's studio. Many admired it, intrigued by the story behind it. But every time Jenny looked at it, she felt a chill, a reminder of that fateful night when she came face to face with the tragic ghost of Bodmin Moor.

The moors hold many secrets, many tales. But Jenny's encounter with Charlotte was a story she would never forget—a poignant reminder of the thin line that separates the living from the dead, love from betrayal, and the haunting beauty of places like Bodmin Moor.

CHAPTER 30:

The Ghosts of Warwick Castle, Warwickshire

The Warwick Castle, set against the River Avon's flow, seemed to defy time itself. A fortress of medieval architecture, its towers reached for the heavens as if in prayer, yet the tales it held within its cold stone walls were anything but holy.

Giles Tremaine, an American historian with a penchant for the obscure, had come to Warwickshire to learn more about its famous castle. As he approached the castle's gates, the grandeur of the place struck him. Yet, even in daylight, shadows seemed to dance at every corner, and the air around him held a heaviness that made him shiver.

He was particularly interested in the Watergate Tower, a central piece of the castle's architecture with a history steeped in intrigue and bloodshed. Locals whispered that Sir Fulke Greville, once a proud owner of the castle, haunted this tower. Giles was not one to shy away from a good ghost story, and the lure of this tale was too potent to resist.

Guided tours were not for Giles. Instead, he'd managed to befriend a castle caretaker named Harold, an old man who'd served the castle for decades. Harold knew every nook and cranny, every hidden chamber, and every whispered tale.

One evening, after the visitors had left and the sun dipped below the horizon, Harold took Giles to the Watergate Tower. The winding staircase seemed endless. With each step, the torches on the walls flickered as if threatened by an unseen wind.

"Sir Fulke, he was an ambitious man," Harold began, his voice echoing through the narrow passageway. "His desire for power and wealth knew no bounds. But it was his trusted servant who turned against him, ending his life in a fit of jealousy and rage."

As they reached the top, Giles looked out of a window. The River Avon flowed quietly below, oblivious to the tales of horror that had played out above its waters.

Harold continued, "They say Sir Fulke's spirit still lingers. He wanders this tower, mourning his untimely death, betrayed by one he held close."

Giles glanced around, trying to imagine the scene. Suddenly, a cold breeze swept through the room, extinguishing the torches. In the dim moonlight, he could make out a faint silhouette. A figure dressed in medieval attire, standing still, its gaze fixed on Giles.

Frozen in fear, Giles watched as the apparition moved closer. A sense of sorrow, regret, and anger emanated from the spirit. The shadowy figure stopped inches from Giles, the details of its face obscured by the darkness.

"Who are you?" Giles managed to croak out.

"I am Fulke," the spirit whispered, its voice filled with anguish. "Betrayed and murdered in my own home."

"What do you want?" Giles asked, his heart pounding.

"Justice," the spirit replied. "My betrayer never faced the consequences of his actions."

Harold, who had been silent until now, spoke up, "Sir Fulke, your time has passed. You must find peace."

The spirit turned its gaze to Harold. "You, caretaker, have been here long. You know the truth."

Giles watched in horror as the apparition moved closer to Harold. The old man stood his ground, defiant. "I know the tales," Harold responded, "but you must let go of your anger. Revenge won't bring you peace."

The spirit seemed to grow taller, its form shifting and contorting. "I will have my vengeance," it roared.

Giles, driven by a sudden surge of courage, stepped forward. "Sir Fulke," he said, "your tale is tragic, and I understand your pain. But continuing this cycle of revenge won't end your suffering."

The room grew colder. The spirit seemed to consider Giles's words. For a moment, there was silence.

Then, the spirit's voice echoed once more, "I am bound to this place, to this tower. Until my murderer's bloodline ends, I will remain."

Harold's face turned ashen. "That bloodline," he whispered, "is mine."

Giles's heart sank. The weight of realization bore down on him. The old caretaker, his newfound friend, was tied to the castle's dark past in a way he could never have imagined.

The spirit's focus shifted to Harold. "Your ancestors took my life," Sir Fulke murmured. "Now, I claim yours."

Before Giles could react, the apparition lunged at Harold. The old man's scream echoed through the tower as darkness consumed them.

When Giles opened his eyes, he was alone. The torches once again flickered on the walls. Of Harold, there was no sign. Only his lantern, dropped in the struggle, its light now extinguished.

The weight of the castle's history pressed down on Giles. The tales of hauntings, the whispers of the locals, they were all true. The Watergate Tower held a darkness that could not be escaped.

Weeks later, Giles would leave Warwickshire, but the memories of that night haunted his dreams. He'd come seeking stories of the past, but he left with a chilling tale of his own – one he'd never forget.

And somewhere in the depths of Warwick Castle, Sir Fulke's spirit continued its restless wanderings, waiting for the next unsuspecting soul to venture into the Watergate Tower.

CHAPTER 31:

The Ghosts of the Theatre Royal, Drury Lane, London

Dusk settled over London, painting the sky with orange and pink hues, fading gradually to a steely grey. The Theatre Royal in Drury Lane, with its ornate façade, stood as an imposing reminder of the city's illustrious past. Tonight, it would bear witness to the premiere of "The Heart's Abyss", an eagerly anticipated play by the up-and-coming playwright, James Winslow.

Inside the theatre, Lydia Carrington, a lead actress, adjusted her gown as she took one final look in the mirror before her debut. She felt a strange chill creep up her spine, causing her to shiver. Dismissing it as mere nerves, she decided to take a walk around the theatre to calm herself.

As Lydia strolled through the quiet corridors, she stumbled upon a painting of a mysterious man draped in grey, eyes haunting and full of sorrow. Intrigued, Lydia was soon lost in the depth of the painting when she felt a touch on her shoulder. Startled, she turned to find nothing but an empty corridor behind her.

"Evening nerves," she whispered to herself.

Elsewhere, the stage manager, Charles Bennett, was having troubles of his own. Props were going missing, lights were flickering, and set pieces were moving on their own. He had heard tales of the Theatre Royal being haunted, particularly by the apparition known as the 'Man in Grey'. However, Charles, a staunch rationalist, scoffed at such stories.

The clock chimed seven, signalling the beginning of the play. As the curtain rose, the audience settled into their seats, rapt with attention.

Yet, as the play progressed, something felt amiss. An unmistakable coldness filled the air, causing the audience to huddle closer together. Whispered conversations began to circulate about the theatre's notorious ghostly resident.

Lydia, lost in her character, failed to notice the subtle changes. Until, during a pivotal scene, a mysterious grey shadow flitted across the stage. Gasps rippled through the audience. She tried to maintain her composure, but a growing sense of unease gnawed at her.

During the interval, Lydia rushed backstage, her heart racing. Charles approached her, his face pale. "Did you see it?" she demanded.

He nodded slowly. "The Man in Grey. I saw him too."

Despite the eerie atmosphere, the two decided the show must go on. They dismissed the cast's anxious chatter, attributing the sightings to overactive imaginations.

As the second act began, the disturbances intensified. Whispers filled the air, as though conversations from another era were echoing through the theatre. Suddenly, the lights dimmed, plunging the stage into darkness. Panic ensued as audience members and cast alike scrambled to find their way out.

Through the pandemonium, Lydia heard a voice, soft and melancholic, singing an old ballad. It emanated from the royal box. As her eyes adjusted to the dark, she saw a figure, draped in grey, watching her intently.

Mustering courage, Lydia approached the box. As she neared, the figure became clearer – it was the same man from the painting. Their eyes met, and in that fleeting moment, a torrent of emotions washed over Lydia – sorrow, loss, and an inexplicable connection.

The 'Man in Grey' reached out, and Lydia, drawn like a moth to a flame, took his hand. Time seemed to stand still as they danced gracefully across the stage, lost in each other's embrace.

Meanwhile, Charles managed to restore the lights, revealing the enigmatic dance to the stunned audience. The theatre echoed with silence, punctuated only by the soft steps of the ethereal dance.

As the music reached its climax, the 'Man in Grey' leaned in, whispering into Lydia's ear. The words were indiscernible to the audience, but Lydia's face turned ashen. With a final spin, he released her, bowing gracefully before vanishing into thin air.

Lydia stood in the centre of the stage, her expression a mixture of terror and realization. The audience, still in shock, slowly began to applaud, believing it to be part of the performance.

But Lydia knew better. The whisper had been a warning, a message from beyond – "Leave this place, for it belongs to us, to the forgotten, to the shadows."

The play concluded to a standing ovation, but the events of the night left a profound impact on Lydia and Charles.

In the days that followed, Lydia, haunted by the encounter, left the theatre and the world of acting altogether. Charles, his scepticism shattered, resigned from his position, vowing never to return to the Theatre Royal.

The legend of the 'Man in Grey' grew, with many speculating about his identity and purpose. Some said he was a protective spirit, while others believed he was bound to the theatre due to a tragic event from his past.

The Theatre Royal, Drury Lane, continued to enchant and terrify its patrons in equal measure. But one thing was for certain – within its walls, the boundary between the living and the dead was perilously thin, and those who dared to tread too close often paid the price.

CHAPTER 32:

The Ghost of Lady Howard, Dartmoor

Dartmoor, a landscape where the moors whispered tales older than time, was no stranger to eerie stories. Yet, among its folktales and whispered legends, none was as chilling as that of Lady Howard.

In the quaint village of Okehampton, nestled on the edge of Dartmoor, lived an old man named Albert. His family had resided there for generations, and like every elder in the village, he was a wellspring of local lore. To those who would listen, Albert would recount tales that had the power to make grown men shiver. Yet, of all his stories, he told the tale of Lady Howard most infrequently and always with a certain trepidation.

It was a dark evening, rain tapping on the windowpanes of the village pub, when a young journalist named Clara, who had travelled from London to cover Dartmoor's beauty and mysteries, overheard murmurs about Lady Howard's legend. Curiosity piqued, she approached Albert.

He eyed her sceptically. "Are you sure you want to hear this tale, lass?"

Clara nodded, and thus Albert began his narrative.

Lady Howard was once the most admired woman in Dartmoor, not just for her beauty but for her vast wealth. Married four times, each of her husbands died under mysterious circumstances, leaving her wealthier with each passing. Whispers of foul play trailed her, but nothing was ever proven.

Yet, her wealth couldn't protect her from a damning rumour: it was said that every night, she would travel from Okehampton Castle to Tavistock and back in a ghastly carriage made entirely of bones – the bones of her dead husbands. A massive spectral hound, said to be as black as the night, accompanied her, its eyes glowing a piercing red. Her task was to pluck a single blade of grass from the moors, a penance for her sins. Only when every blade was plucked - which would essentially mean the end of the world - would she find peace.

Clara, though entranced, scoffed lightly. "It's just a tale," she whispered to herself.

Albert leaned in, his voice a low growl. "Many have thought so, till they've seen her. The carriage, the hound... and the Lady, her face white as death, her eyes filled with eternal torment."

Determined to validate or debunk the story, Clara decided to venture out to the moors that night. Albert, against his better judgment, agreed to guide her, warning that they'd keep their distance.

They set out, the vast Dartmoor moors stretching endlessly, the wind howling its mournful tune. Hours passed with no sign of the ghostly carriage. The cold began to seep into Clara's bones, and doubt clouded her determination.

But then, as midnight approached, a thick fog rolled in. An oppressive silence enveloped the moors. Albert clutched his coat tight, his eyes darting around. "We should leave," he whispered.

Before Clara could respond, a distant sound echoed – the clatter of hooves and the creak of wheels. The noise grew louder, and through the fog, a bone carriage emerged, drawn by skeletal horses. Beside it ran a massive black hound, its eyes a haunting shade of red. Inside the carriage, an ethereal figure with a veil stared blankly ahead - Lady Howard.

Frozen in fear, Clara could only watch as the carriage stopped not far from them. Lady Howard stepped out, her movements graceful yet ghostly. She approached a patch of grass and, kneeling, plucked a single blade. Then, with a wail that chilled the very soul, she re-entered the carriage, which vanished into the fog as quickly as it had appeared.

Albert, pale as a sheet, grabbed Clara's arm. "We need to leave, now!"

As they hurriedly made their way back, the haunting wail of Lady Howard echoed in the distance, a reminder of her endless torment.

Back in the safety of the pub, Clara, still reeling, penned down her experience. The story would become her most acclaimed piece, earning her numerous accolades.

Yet, fame came at a price. Every night, Clara would dream of the moors, of the bone carriage, and of Lady Howard's piercing eyes staring into her very soul. No matter where she went, the scent of the moors and the distant sound of hooves followed her.

One evening, Clara returned to Dartmoor, compelled by an unseen force. She was found the next morning, sitting motionless on the moors, a single blade of grass clutched in her hand. Her eyes, once lively, now mirrored the same torment she had seen in Lady Howard's.

Albert, hearing of Clara's fate, could only sigh. Dartmoor had claimed another soul. And as for Lady Howard, her nightly journey continues, a chilling reminder of the thin line between legend and reality.

For in Dartmoor, tales aren't just tales. They are memories, they are warnings, and, sometimes, they are destinies waiting to unfold.

CHAPTER 33:

The Ghosts of the Banqueting House, London

On the chilly night of January 29th, the dim gas lamps of London threw distorted, angular shadows onto the cobbled streets. Michael, a young writer with jet-black hair and a penchant for history, stood outside the gates of the Banqueting House, the only remaining part of Whitehall Palace. His hands trembled as he sketched the edifice's facade, trying to capture its stark beauty. Little did he know that he was about to become a part of its haunted history.

Earlier that day, Michael had received a mysterious letter, sent by an anonymous source. The elegant script inside spoke of an unpublished manuscript, a firsthand account of King Charles I's final moments before his execution at the Banqueting House. As a history enthusiast, Michael couldn't resist the allure. The letter instructed him to be at the Banqueting House at midnight, where he would find the manuscript hidden.

The massive door creaked open just a touch as he approached, an invitation or a forewarning, Michael couldn't tell. He stepped inside, and the outside noises immediately hushed, replaced by an eerie silence that made his heart beat louder in his ears.

The main hall was cavernous, with ornate ceilings painted by the master Rubens himself. The soft light from the chandeliers gave the room a golden glow, but it was the large wooden platform in the middle that captured Michael's attention. An exact spot where King Charles I had been executed.

Michael approached it hesitantly, his boots echoing on the polished marble floor. As he got closer, the temperature dropped dramatically, making him shiver. On the platform, he found an old leather-bound book, exactly where the letter said it would be. He reached out to grab it, but the moment he touched it, a gust of cold wind blew through the hall, extinguishing all the lights.

Panicking, Michael fumbled for a match. When he managed to light one, the little flame revealed a figure standing on the platform—King Charles I, his royal garments torn and bloody, his eyes hollow and his head, eerily, was tucked under his arm.

Frozen in terror, Michael watched as the ghostly king reenacted his final moments. The spectral crowd jeered, and the axe gleamed before descending with a sickening thud. The scene played over and over like a broken record. Each time, King Charles' eyes met Michael's, pleading, accusing.

Trying to break the loop, Michael yelled out, "I'm not one of them! I'm not responsible for your death!"

Suddenly, the scene changed. The Banqueting House transformed into a lavish feast. Ghostly figures danced and laughed, toasting to the King's demise. Michael found himself seated at the head of the table, but before he could react, hands grabbed him from behind, pinning him to the chair. The ghostly figures turned their attention to him, their cheers becoming menacing. They thrust a crown upon his head, mockingly naming him the new king.

In the midst of his terror, Michael noticed another figure—separate from the rest, a woman draped in a black veil, her face obscured. She approached him slowly, whispering, "You've seen too much. You mustn't leave."

As she drew closer, the air became icy. The spectral attendees' laughter grew more sinister. Michael felt the weight of history, of all those who had met gruesome ends within these walls, pressing down on him. Desperate, he threw the manuscript into the air. The room plunged into darkness once again.

When the lights returned, Michael found himself outside the Banqueting House, the early morning sun painting the streets of London in golden hues. The massive doors were shut tight, with no sign of the horrors he had just witnessed.

Shaken, he hurried home. When he tried to write about his experience, his words twisted on the page, turning into pleas for forgiveness from the long-dead king. No matter how many times he tried, the outcome was always the same.

Weeks turned into months, and Michael became a recluse, haunted by the eyes of King Charles I. Every night, he would wake up to the ghostly reenactment of the execution, the axe falling, the king's eyes accusing.

He sought the help of mediums, priests, and scholars, but none could free him from the king's grasp. They all advised him to leave London, but he couldn't. Every time he tried, an unseen force would pull him back.

On the anniversary of that fateful night, Michael returned to the Banqueting House one last time. The doors opened, welcoming him into the darkness. The next morning, a groundskeeper found the same leather-bound manuscript on the execution platform.

The final entry read, "Let history remember the weight of its actions, lest they be repeated. I have paid for my curiosity, becoming a prisoner of the past. Beware, for the Banqueting House does not forget or forgive."

And so, Michael's tale became yet another dark chapter in the haunted history of the Banqueting House. If you ever find yourself wandering the streets of London at night, avoid the shadow of the Banqueting House, or you too might become a part of its ghostly tapestry.

CHAPTER 34:

The Ghost of the Lady in Green, Thetford Priory, Norfolk

In the dim light of dawn, when mist meandered over the ruins of the Cluniac Priory of Our Lady of Thetford, Norfolk's once-grand testament to faith was now no more than crumbled bricks, decaying altars, and stories that made the bravest shiver.

Paul, an ambitious photographer, was consumed by passion for capturing the unseen and the forgotten. He'd heard of Thetford Priory's eerie allure, how it seduced visitors into its shadows with tales of a hooded monk and a mysterious Lady in Green. He thought a few haunting snaps of the ruins at dawn might fetch a pretty penny or, better still, make the cover of some national magazine.

He parked his car a distance away, walking the remaining stretch to feel the pulse of the old earth underfoot. As he approached, the hush of the morning was shattered by the distant song of a thrush. Paul's footsteps were muffled by the damp grass, his breath fogging in the early chill.

Setting up his tripod and camera, he aimed at the main archway, fingers working deftly to adjust the settings. He clicked a few times, capturing the structure in the slowly brightening light.

Then he noticed something peculiar. On the playback screen, standing amidst the archway, was a shadowy figure that wasn't there moments before. He blinked, figuring it was a trick of the light, or perhaps his eyes were playing tricks on him from the morning haze. Deleting the image, he looked up to take another shot.

But as the seconds passed, Paul felt an unexplainable chill run down his spine. The ruins felt less welcoming now. The morning songs of birds had quieted, replaced by an unnatural silence.

Eager to finish, he repositioned for another shot when he heard a faint whisper carried by the wind, "Why have you come?"

Paul whipped around, searching for the source. But there was no one.

Suddenly, a soft, melodious humming filled the air, echoing across the open space. It had an ancient lilt, a lament that seemed to tell of love lost and promises unfulfilled. As Paul scanned the ruins, his eyes landed on a figure slowly materializing in the distance.

She was a vision, draped in an ethereal green gown that flowed with the breeze. Long, raven-black hair cascaded down her back. Her eyes, however, told of tragedies too painful for words. They were eyes that had seen centuries pass.

The Lady in Green beckoned him with a porcelain hand, her lips curved in a sad smile. Paul, for reasons he couldn't fathom, felt compelled to approach.

As he drew nearer, the air grew colder, and the ground beneath seemed to tremble. The Lady in Green spoke, her voice an echo from a time long past.

"Why have you come? Do you wish to hear my tale?"

Paul hesitated, sensing the danger. But the allure of her voice, the story she promised, was too much. He nodded.

"My love and I were to wed, but before we could, the monastery fell to ruins, and he took vows as a monk. Heartbroken, I too sought solace in faith, but we couldn't keep away from each other. One night, under the moon's gentle glow, we met here, in secret. But our tryst was discovered, and as punishment, he was sealed alive within the walls of the priory. I was left to roam, forever seeking him."

Paul's pulse quickened. "That's tragic, but why are you telling me this?"

Her gaze deepened, and her fingers ghosted over his cheek. "Because every century, a man stumbles upon my ruins, and I need him to set me free. To break the curse, to be reunited with my love. Will you help me?"

Mesmerized, Paul could only nod.

The Lady in Green pointed to a particular spot amidst the ruins. "Behind that wall, my love awaits. Free him, and I shall be free."

Paul approached the indicated wall. The bricks were old and weathered, crumbled by time. With bare hands, he began to tear them away, each brick weighing heavily with the sorrow of the Lady's tale.

Hours seemed to pass, and finally, he reached a cavity. Within, he found a skeleton draped in the remains of monk's robes. Beside it, an old, faded letter.

Paul picked it up, reading the words written in anguish.

"To my love,

If you ever find this, know that my last thoughts were of you. I hope one day we will be reunited in another life, free from these earthly chains.

Forever yours."

A shiver ran down Paul's spine. The reality of what he had unearthed, the weight of the tragedy, pressed down on him. He turned back to the Lady in Green, expecting gratitude.

But what he saw made his blood run cold.

The Lady in Green, once ethereal and beautiful, now appeared twisted and tormented. Her gown was tattered, her face aged and wretched. Her fingers, gnarled and bony, reached out to him.

"You've freed him," she hissed, her voice a chilling rasp. "Now, you must take his place."

Paul stumbled back in horror, his screams echoing through the ruins. As her fingers brushed his arm, he felt a coldness seep into his very soul. The world around him began to blur and fade.

The next morning, the Priory stood silent, its secrets held close. A camera lay abandoned near the archway. And amidst the ruins, if one listened closely, they could hear the faint, agonizing wails of a soul trapped in eternal torment.

As for the Lady in Green and her monk, they were finally reunited, wandering the ruins hand in hand, their tragic love story a cautionary tale for all who dared to tread on hallowed ground.

CHAPTER 35:

The Ghost of Sker House

Wales, with its rich Celtic history and vast landscapes, is home to many a tale of ghosts and phantoms. Sker House, a sprawling 12th-century mansion in Bridgend, stands as a silent testimony to one such haunting legend. The core of this story revolves around a heartrending tale of forbidden love, betrayal, and an insatiable thirst for revenge.

Matthew Davis, an aspiring writer in his late twenties, had just received a commission to document the haunting legends across Britain. Sker House was next on his list. Eager to experience the ghostly tales firsthand, he decided to spend a few nights at the mansion.

The locals warned him. No one stayed overnight at Sker House anymore. It was the domain of Elizabeth Williams, or so the legend went. A young woman whose love story had met a tragic end in those very halls. Ignoring their words, Matthew, a firm sceptic, armed with only a typewriter and a lantern, entered the mansion.

As he roamed the echoing chambers of Sker House, the weight of its history pressed down on him. Centuries of stories whispered from the stone walls, but none was louder than that of Elizabeth.

Elizabeth Williams was the beautiful daughter of Isaac Williams, the then-owner of Sker House in the 1800s. She fell in love with a shipwrecked sailor named Thomas Evans. Her father disapproved, wanting her to marry a man of wealth. When Elizabeth refused to relent, she was locked in one of the mansion's rooms, condemned to a life of solitude.

One evening, as the sun dipped below the horizon, casting long, ominous shadows across the mansion's interiors, Matthew decided to set up his typewriter in that very room.

The silence was palpable, broken only by the rhythmic clacking of his typewriter. Hours seemed to meld into one another until a soft, forlorn humming broke his concentration. He looked around, half-expecting to find a source for the sound, but found none.

Shrugging it off as fatigue, he decided to head to bed. He chose a room overlooking the moors. As he settled into the cold, hard bed, the melancholic humming resumed, but this time, accompanied by a shadow dancing on his window pane.

Curiosity piqued, Matthew peered outside, but there was no one. Just the vast, untouched moors bathed in moonlight. As he turned back, he caught sight of a fleeting image in the hallway. A young woman in a flowing white dress, her face pale and eyes sorrowful. She was there one moment and gone the next.

Sleep evaded Matthew that night.

The next morning, determined to get to the root of the haunting, Matthew decided to explore the mansion further.

In the attic, he stumbled upon an old, dust-covered diary. Its pages yellowed with age and written in a delicate hand, it was Elizabeth's.

Page after page, her tormented life unfurled before him. Her love for Thomas, her father's wrath, and her eventual tragic demise in the very room she was imprisoned in.

As night approached, Matthew was once again drawn to that room. Sitting in the dim light, he began to type, reciting Elizabeth's tale. With each word, the atmosphere grew denser. The humming grew louder, more desperate, echoing the pain and torment Elizabeth had endured.

Suddenly, the door slammed shut, plunging the room into darkness. The lantern flickered, casting eerie shadows on the walls. Matthew felt a cold presence, and a whisper caressed his ear, "Help me."

Frantically, he tried the door, but it wouldn't budge. Panic surged through him. The air grew colder, and the humming morphed into a haunting lullaby. The shadows danced violently, converging to form a figure—the ghostly apparition of Elizabeth Williams.

Her eyes, once full of life, were now hollow, her face twisted in anguish. "Why did they forsake me?" she wailed, her voice echoing in the darkness.

Matthew, paralyzed with fear, managed to whisper, "Elizabeth?"

In response, the room seemed to come alive. The walls appeared to close in, and the haunting melody of her life filled the air. He saw flashes of her life—her meeting with

Thomas, their stolen moments, and her final heart-wrenching days locked away.

Then, just as suddenly as it began, it ended. The room was back to normal. But the weight of Elizabeth's sorrow was palpable.

Dawn broke, bringing with it the promise of a new day. Matthew, now a firm believer in the supernatural, packed his belongings. He had gotten more than he bargained for at Sker House.

As he stepped outside, the vast moors seemed to breathe a sigh of relief. The mansion, with all its tales, stood silent and imposing, a sentinel to Elizabeth's tale of woe.

But as Matthew looked back one last time, he could swear he saw the fleeting image of a young woman, standing at the window, her face sorrowful, eyes searching, forever waiting for her lost love.

Haunted Britain had a new chilling tale to add to its chronicles, one that whispered of undying love and eternal sorrow. A tale that proved love, even in death, could never truly be silenced.

CHAPTER 36:

The Ghost of Richard III in Leicester

Leicester, a city filled with history, culture, and bustling streets, was also home to a secret most of its inhabitants were unaware of. Beneath the grey asphalt of a car park, the past lay waiting, a monarch buried without the pomp and honour he was due.

Tom Grant, an archaeologist in his mid-thirties, had just landed the project of a lifetime. His team had been granted permission to excavate a section of the city car park rumoured to house the remains of Richard III, the last English king to die in battle.

On the first day of the excavation, there was excitement in the air. News crews hovered, capturing the historic moment. Tom's hands shook as he peeled back the earth, layers upon layers of history coming off with each shovel.

By the third day, they had found it - a skeleton. A curved spine was the giveaway. Richard III, long rumoured to be a hunchback, lay there, waiting to be rediscovered. But that wasn't all. A chill ran down Tom's spine as he realized the skull bore a deep wound, evidence of a fatal blow.

While the discovery should've been the pinnacle of Tom's career, dark clouds began to form over the project.

It began with small occurrences. Equipment malfunctioned. Precious artifacts disappeared. Crew members reported nightmares of a bloodied king chasing them through the mists of Bosworth Field, his face twisted in rage, his hands reaching out to strangle them.

It escalated when crew member Jenny, a bright young student of archaeology, was found on site one morning, her face white as chalk. She whispered of shadows that whispered back and of a cold hand that had gripped her ankle in the dead of night. She resigned the next day.

Tom tried to stay rational. Mass hysteria, he told himself. The weight of the discovery, the pressure of the media. But then, it happened to him.

He was working late one evening, piecing together remnants of pottery, when he felt it - a cold gust of wind in the enclosed tent. The candles flickered, and the hairs on the back of his neck stood upright. A shadow, long and twisted, crept across the tent wall. A whisper, thin as a reed, reached his ears.

"Why hast thou disturbed me?"

Tom froze. The voice, deep and gravelly, echoed in his head. He wanted to flee, but his legs wouldn't respond.

The temperature in the tent dropped further. Objects began to levitate – shards of pottery, tools, even the heavy wooden table shook. Tom felt the grip of unseen fingers around his throat, squeezing the air out of him.

He fought against the force, choking, gasping, feeling consciousness slip away, when suddenly, everything stopped. The objects fell. The whispering ceased. Tom, drenched in sweat, found himself alone in the quiet tent.

The next day, he called in a local priest, Father James, known for his knowledge on exorcisms and the paranormal. Father James listened quietly, his face pale but attentive.

"The spirit of Richard III is restless," Father James whispered. "He died a violent death, lost to history, vilified by Shakespeare. Now that you've uncovered him, he seeks acknowledgment. He wants his due."

Tom nodded. "So, what do we do?"

"You need to give him a proper burial," Father James replied, "With all the honour he deserves. Only then will he be at peace."

Preparations began for a royal reburial at the Leicester Cathedral. The city was alive with activity, and historians from around the world arrived to witness the event.

The night before the ceremony, Tom decided to stay overnight at the excavation site, feeling a sense of duty to the restless spirit.

Hours into the night, he was awakened by a noise. Opening his eyes, he found himself face to face with the apparition of Richard III. His skeletal face, translucent in the moonlight, bore an expression of sadness, not the rage Tom had experienced before.

Richard's ghostly form extended a bony finger, pointing towards the burial site, then to the Cathedral, and lastly, to his own heart. His mouth opened, but instead of words, a mournful wail escaped, echoing into the night, sending a shiver down Tom's spine.

The message was clear. Acknowledge the heart, the soul, and give it its rightful place.

The next morning, with the sun shining bright and the city gathered, Richard III was given a burial fit for a king. Tom, standing at the forefront, felt a weight lift off his shoulders. As the final words were spoken, he thought he saw, just for a moment, the ghostly figure of Richard, nodding in approval and slowly fading away.

The city of Leicester returned to its regular rhythm, its secrets buried deep. But Tom Grant knew that some things, once uncovered, would never be the same.

That night, as the city celebrated, Tom, in his hotel room, heard a whisper, softer this time, almost grateful.

"Now, I can finally rest."

The tale of Richard III's ghost became another chapter in the rich tapestry of Leicester's history. The city flourished, and Tom went on with his life. But every once in a while, when the wind blew cold and the moon shone bright, the ghostly whisper of a fallen king could still be heard, reminding the living of debts owed to the dead.

CHAPTER 37:

The Haunting of the Jamaica Inn, Cornwall

Cornwall, 1984.

The old, twisted road that led to the Jamaica Inn was notorious for its fog. A thick, oppressive fog that would appear from nowhere, swallowing up all light and sound. On this particular night, it lay dense upon the landscape, muffling the sounds of nocturnal animals and obscuring the moon's glow.

Jenna, a budding journalist from London, had heard of the stories surrounding the Jamaica Inn. She decided to visit, intent on debunking the alleged ghostly encounters and give a logical explanation for the tales of phantom footsteps and apparitional smugglers that guests at the inn frequently spoke of.

She parked her car, its headlights barely piercing the fog, and stepped out into the cool night air. The mist wrapped around her like a clammy hand, and she felt a shiver travel up her spine. Dismissing it as just the chill, she grabbed her bags and headed to the entrance.

The inn itself seemed to materialize out of the fog as she approached, looming large and ominous, its ancient stone walls seeming to whisper of secrets long kept. The entrance door creaked loudly as she opened it, announcing her arrival to the few patrons sitting at the bar, nursing their drinks.

"Evening," said the bartender, an older man with deep-set eyes and greying hair. "You're brave, coming here on such a night."

Jenna smiled. "I've heard the stories. I'm here to see for myself if they're true."

The bartender raised an eyebrow. "Most come to escape the tales, not to seek them."

She chuckled. "Just need a room and a good night's sleep. Got a busy day tomorrow."

He handed her a key with the number '7' on it. "Second floor, end of the corridor. Sleep well."

Jenna found her room without incident, her footsteps echoing on the wooden floorboards. The room was rustic, with heavy wooden beams and a large, ornate bed. It seemed cozy enough, and she quickly settled in.

She had almost drifted off to sleep when she heard it. A soft whisper, like cloth brushing against cloth, then footsteps. Barely audible, they seemed to be coming from the hallway. Jenna sat up, her heart pounding. She told herself it was probably just another guest. Yet, she felt an unease she couldn't shake off.

She slipped out of bed and tiptoed to the door, pressing her ear against it. The footsteps were closer now, accompanied by a faint murmuring. Unable to resist her curiosity, she cautiously opened the door a crack.

The corridor was empty.

The footsteps continued, growing louder, but there was no one in sight. Jenna's heart raced as she realized the sound was coming from beneath the floorboards. She thought of the tales, the smugglers who used hidden tunnels beneath the inn, and a cold dread settled in her stomach.

Suddenly, a chilling wind blew through the corridor, extinguishing the candles lining the walls. The inn plunged into darkness. Jenna stumbled back into her room, slamming the door shut. The murmuring grew louder, more distinct, sounding like hushed conversations between several people.

She fumbled for her flashlight and shone it around the room. Nothing seemed amiss. Just as she began to convince herself she'd imagined it all, she saw something that froze her blood.

A shadowy figure, translucent and flickering, stood at the foot of her bed. It was a man, with wild, unkempt hair and a ragged coat, staring right at her with hollow eyes. Behind him, more figures began to materialize, each more menacing than the last. They were murmuring, discussing something in hushed tones.

"Who are you?" Jenna whispered, her voice trembling.

The lead figure pointed to the ground beneath her. "Smugglers," he hissed. "Betrayed. Murdered. Buried."

Jenna's mind raced. The stories she'd heard of ghostly smugglers weren't just tales. They were real. And they were here.

"Why are you here?" she managed to ask.

The figure's hollow eyes bore into hers. "Seeking justice. Seeking retribution."

Jenna felt a pressure building in the room, a tension that felt like it would explode at any moment. The ghostly figures were closing in on her, their murmurs growing louder, more insistent.

She felt a hand close around her ankle, cold and clammy. Panicking, she tried to pull away, but more hands grabbed her, pulling her down. She screamed, but no sound came out. The room seemed to spin as the hands dragged her towards the floor, the wooden planks giving way beneath her.

She fell into darkness, the murmurs of the smugglers echoing in her ears. The last thing she heard before everything went silent was the chilling voice of the lead figure.

"Justice has been served."

The next morning, the inn's cleaning lady knocked on Jenna's door. When there was no response, she entered, finding the room empty. The bed was neatly made, and there was no sign of the young journalist.

The inn's patrons whispered among themselves, wondering what had happened to the curious woman from

London. Some said she'd left in the middle of the night, spooked by the tales. Others weren't so sure.

The bartender, however, looked at room number '7', a troubled expression on his face. He remembered another guest, many years ago, who had also disappeared without a trace from that very room.

He thought of the tales, of the smugglers betrayed and murdered, their bodies hidden in the tunnels below. And he couldn't help but wonder if Jenna had found the truth of the Jamaica Inn – a truth that would forever remain buried beneath its ancient floorboards.

CHAPTER 38:

The Grey Lady of Glamis Castle, Scotland

The imposing stone structure of Glamis Castle stood as an ageless sentinel against the backdrop of Scotland's rolling green hills. For centuries, it had been the ancestral home of the Earls of Strathmore, and with its history came the tales of those who never left—even in death.

Sarah, a researcher of old Scottish tales and folklore, had travelled from Edinburgh to the castle on a chilly autumn day. She was curious about one tale in particular: the legend of the Grey Lady. Not just a mere apparition, but the wandering spirit of Lady Janet Douglas. Whispered rumours swirled around her unjust death, and how her very soul could not find peace.

In the local tavern, as Sarah prepared for her trip to the castle, she overheard the old barman, Angus, speak in hushed tones with a patron. "They say she looks for justice...for someone to set right what was wrong."

Sarah approached Angus curiously. "Excuse me, sir. Might you know anything about the Grey Lady?"

Angus's old eyes looked deep into Sarah's. "Aye, lass. The Lady Janet was accused of witchcraft and treason, a false claim, many believe. They say she was betrayed and sentenced to die, burned right at Edinburgh Castle. And now, her spirit wanders her old home, a grey spectre of sadness."

Sarah's heart raced. "Has anyone seen her recently?"

Angus hesitated. "Few live to tell the tale. Those who do… they're never the same."

Glamis Castle was as grand as it was eerie. As Sarah walked the cold, echoing halls, the portraits on the walls seemed to watch her every move. The weight of history pressed down on her. Every creak of the wood, every gust of wind made her heart jump.

On the second night of her stay, as the last rays of the sun disappeared beyond the horizon and the castle was enveloped in darkness, Sarah decided to venture to the chambers of Lady Janet. The room was preserved as it was when she lived, a haunting memorial to the castle's tragic resident.

With only a candle to guide her, Sarah's footsteps echoed through the vast corridors. As she approached the room, a sudden cold draft blew out her candle. In the inky blackness, she felt a presence. Her breath became shallow, and a paralyzing fear took over her.

From the darkness, a soft voice whispered, "Who enters my chamber?"

Sarah, trembling, managed to utter, "I'm here to learn your story, to understand your pain."

A dim light began to glow, illuminating the spectral figure of a woman dressed in grey. Her eyes were pools of sorrow, and the aura around her was one of profound sadness. "You seek my tale?"

Sarah nodded, her voice barely audible. "Yes."

The ghost of Lady Janet began her lament. "Betrayed by those I loved, accused of sins I did not commit. My soul is bound to this castle, seeking justice, seeking someone to listen, to understand."

Sarah, tears in her eyes, replied, "I will listen."

As the hours waned, Lady Janet recounted the betrayal, the false accusations, and the agonizing death she endured. Sarah listened, horrified and saddened. She felt the weight of Lady Janet's despair.

Dawn approached, and the spectral figure began to fade. "Thank you for listening," she whispered, her voice trailing off.

But the air grew colder, and another presence emerged from the shadows. It was malevolent, dark—a stark contrast to Lady Janet. Sarah felt its anger and hatred, a force so strong it threatened to consume her.

Suddenly, Lady Janet's voice rang out, filled with power and urgency. "Run, child! Run from this place!"

Sarah, driven by primal fear, ran through the castle's corridors, her footsteps echoing through the cold stone halls. She could feel the dark presence chasing her, its rage palpable.

She stumbled and fell in front of a large mirror. As she looked up, the reflection wasn't her own. Instead, she saw the distorted face of the one who had betrayed Lady Janet, his eyes filled with anger and madness.

Sarah screamed, scrambling to her feet, and continued her frantic escape. She felt hands reaching out to her from the walls, trying to pull her back into the darkness.

Finally, she burst out of the castle's main doors, the early morning light blinding her. Panting and dishevelled, she looked back at the looming structure. The malevolent force had not followed her outside.

As Sarah walked away from Glamis Castle, she realized she had been given a glimpse into the deep, dark well of human cruelty and betrayal. The tragedy of Lady Janet and the malevolence of her betrayer would haunt Sarah's dreams for years to come.

But more than that, she had felt the indomitable spirit of Lady Janet—a soul forever wandering, forever seeking justice, forever reminding the living of the high price of betrayal.

And so, as the sun cast long shadows across the land, Sarah departed, leaving behind the haunted halls of Glamis Castle and the spectre of the Grey Lady, a tragic reminder of the past's chilling grip on the present.

CHAPTER 39:

The Ghost of the Green Lady, Stirling Castle, Scotland

Ian MacDougall had always been something of a sceptic. Even in Scotland, a land blanketed with centuries-old tales of ghosts, monsters, and other things that go bump in the night, he had managed to grow up dismissive of the legends. It wasn't that he didn't appreciate a good story; he simply couldn't wrap his head around the idea of spirits wandering the earth.

However, his recent assignment as a conservationist at Stirling Castle had been a test of that scepticism.

Stirling Castle, a grand old fortress with towering walls and impressive battlements, was an iconic site in Scotland's rich history. But with its majestic beauty came whispered tales. At first, Ian waved away the old wives' tales of the mysterious Green Lady haunting the castle's drafty halls. But four months into his work, even he couldn't deny the odd occurrences that seemed to plague the castle.

The first incident took place late one evening when Ian had stayed behind to finish some paperwork. The castle was silent, save for the wind that howled through its stone corridors. As he was about to leave, a cold gust enveloped the room, making the candles flicker wildly. The shadows it cast made it seem as if the walls themselves were moving. Ian felt the hair on the back of his neck rise when he noticed a fleeting green hue in the corner of his eye.

Shaking off the unease, he attributed it to exhaustion and left. But the following nights only solidified the feeling of being watched. There was a presence, a weight in the atmosphere that Ian couldn't quite place.

One evening, as a thick fog settled over the castle grounds, Ian found himself in conversation with Mrs. McLintock, the elderly tour guide who had been working at the castle for decades.

"You must have heard about her, lad," she whispered, her eyes gleaming in the dim light. "The Green Lady, the guardian spirit of Stirling Castle."

Ian smirked. "Come now, Mrs. McLintock. Surely you don't believe in such tales?"

Her gaze didn't waver. "It's said she was a servant girl in the castle, during the reign of Mary, Queen of Scots. She was closest to the queen, always by her side. One night, the queen's chambers caught fire. The Green Lady rushed in, saving Mary but perishing in the flames. Now, her spirit roams the castle, ensuring those within its walls are safe."

"An interesting story, no doubt. But just a story."

Mrs. McLintock's eyes twinkled, almost mischievously. "Many have seen her, Ian. She isn't just a tale."

Later that night, while working in one of the chambers, Ian felt a sudden drop in temperature. Shivering, he reached for his jacket, but what he saw next froze him in place. A figure, bathed in a soft green glow, hovered in the doorway. Her silhouette was that of a young woman in a flowing dress, her features indistinct but her eyes—those eyes were pools of deep sadness and longing.

For a moment, they locked gazes. Then, just as suddenly as she had appeared, the apparition vanished.

Ian's scepticism was shattered. The reality of the Green Lady's presence became even more undeniable over the following weeks. Doors creaked open and shut on their own; soft whispers echoed through the halls, and that chilling green hue appeared more frequently, especially during the late hours.

One fateful night, as a storm raged outside, Ian was once again working late in the castle. The wind howled, rain lashed at the windows, and the castle seemed more alive than ever. Distracted by his work, Ian didn't notice the room's temperature drop.

But he did notice when his desk was suddenly illuminated in a soft green light. Looking up, he met the Green Lady's gaze once again. However, this time she seemed more solid, more real. The sadness in her eyes had been replaced with urgency.

Suddenly, the ground beneath Ian trembled. The old walls of the castle groaned and creaked as the quake intensified. The room around him was collapsing!

Ian could barely comprehend what was happening. The ceiling began to crack, debris falling all around him. But then, through the chaos, he felt a cold hand grip his wrist, pulling him away from the imminent collapse.

As the dust settled, Ian found himself outside the chamber, miraculously unharmed. The room he had been in mere moments ago was buried under rubble.

And standing beside him, fading away, was the ethereal figure of the Green Lady. Her eyes, once filled with sadness, now radiated gratitude. With one last lingering look, she disappeared, leaving Ian to grapple with the reality of the supernatural salvation he'd just experienced.

Word of the incident spread, and Ian became something of a local legend. But more than fame or recognition, the event instilled in him a newfound respect for the castle and its ethereal protector. The Green Lady wasn't just a ghost story to frighten children or attract tourists. She was a guardian, forever intertwined with the history and walls of Stirling Castle.

While Ian still had trouble comprehending the supernatural, he could no longer deny the existence of forces beyond understanding. And as the years went by, and he took on a more prominent role within the castle's upkeep, he often found himself working late into the night, always with a small green candle by his side, in tribute to the castle's eternal protector.

CHAPTER 40:

The Phantom Drummer of Edinburgh Castle, Scotland

In the heart of Edinburgh, atop the rocky crag known as Castle Rock, sat Edinburgh Castle. An ancient fortress, it had witnessed centuries of bloodshed, betrayal, and intrigue. Time had etched countless tales into its stone walls, but few as chilling as that of the Phantom Drummer.

Neil Crawford, a historian with a penchant for the esoteric, had decided to spend the summer in Scotland, tracing the remnants of forgotten legends. Edinburgh Castle, with its layers of history, was naturally at the top of his list.

Arriving at the castle on a day blanketed in fog, Neil felt an immediate and inexplicable sense of unease. Every echo of his footsteps on the cobblestone paths seemed to be answered by softer, more distant ones. A trick of the acoustics, surely.

That evening, after a day spent combing through the castle's annals, Neil retired to his lodgings – a small inn close to the castle grounds. The innkeeper, an old Scot named Malcolm, was a treasure trove of local lore.

While nursing his whisky at the inn's bar, Neil mentioned the echoing footsteps. Malcolm's face lost colour. "Ah, lad," he began, "Ye might've heard tales of ghosts and ghouls, but none chill the bone like that of the Phantom Drummer."

As Malcolm narrated, the drummer was a young boy, no more than 16, conscripted against his will to serve as the castle's drummer during one of its many sieges. His beats were the heartbeat of the castle, signalling attacks or retreats.

One fateful night, the boy discovered a plot by a group of treacherous soldiers planning to surrender the castle to the enemy. He tried to warn the captain but was captured by the traitors before he could. They sealed him alive within the walls of the castle, his only companion his drum. For days, muffled drumbeats resonated through the castle, growing weaker with each passing hour until they stopped altogether.

Now, it's said that before calamity strikes the castle or its inhabitants, the ghostly beats of a drum echo through its corridors, a desperate warning from the world beyond.

Neil's logical mind scoffed at the tale, attributing it to the overactive imagination of generations past. Yet, as he settled into his bed that night, he couldn't shake off a feeling of dread.

His unease only grew the next day when he overheard a conservation between two castle guards. Both swore they'd heard faint drumming the previous night, originating from within the walls of the castle's oldest wing.

Curiosity piqued, Neil decided to explore the castle after dark. Armed with a torch and a map of the castle, he ventured into the abandoned corridors of the ancient wing.

The world seemed to shift as Neil delved deeper. The air grew colder, and the shadows darker. As he navigated a particularly narrow hallway, he paused, hearing a faint sound. A rhythmic beating, like that of a... drum.

His heart racing, Neil traced the sound to a dead-end corridor with a lone door. The drumming grew louder, more insistent, pulsating in his ears, as if beckoning him. Swallowing hard, he pushed open the door.

Inside, he was met with pitch darkness. But it wasn't the darkness that made his blood run cold; it was the sudden and complete silence. The drumming had ceased. Neil's torch flickered, illuminating the room in erratic bursts. The walls seemed closer than they should be, as if they were breathing. And then, a sight that froze Neil in place: a skeletal hand, still clutching a battered drumstick, protruding from a crack in the wall.

As realization dawned, a chilling wind blew through the room, extinguishing the torch. Panicking, Neil tried to find the door, but his hands met only solid stone walls. The walls seemed to close in on him, the air thick with centuries of anguish.

And then, the drumming began again, louder and more frantic than before. But it wasn't coming from the walls. It was inside his head. A voice, spectral and mournful, whispered in the dark, "Join me."

Days later, when Neil didn't check out from the inn, Malcolm accompanied the police to Edinburgh Castle. In the ancient wing, they found a door ajar. Pushing it open, they found Neil's lifeless body, eyes wide in terror, clutching his bleeding ears, a battered old drum lying beside him.

The castle's dark legend had claimed another soul.

As the news spread, the townsfolk murmured amongst themselves. While the world saw an unfortunate accident, they knew better. The Phantom Drummer had issued his spectral warning once again. And as always, tragedy wasn't far behind.

Edinburgh Castle, with its panoramic views and rich history, continued to stand tall, drawing visitors from all corners. But those who knew its darker tales approached with caution, ever wary of the faint, eerie drumbeats echoing through its ancient halls.

CHAPTER 41:

The Headless Phantom of Hever Castle, Kent

The ancient, turreted silhouette of Hever Castle stretched up against the blood-red horizon, casting long shadows over the velvet green of Kent. It was a formidable sight, one that commanded respect and a touch of dread.

The setting sun left a trail of indigo, and in that twilight, the castle became a place of old memories and older regrets. The ornate windows looked down upon its grounds like so many judgmental eyes, and the wind carried secrets whispered by the ghosts of its past.

Among those whispered tales was the one of Anne Boleyn, the beautiful and ambitious woman who won and lost a king's heart. Her life was a tapestry of love, betrayal, and tragedy, ending in her untimely execution.

Sarah, a young historian with a deep interest in the Tudor period, had come to Hever Castle to delve deeper into Anne's life. It was her first assignment for the reputed journal "Historical Echoes." Armed with her notepad, camera, and relentless curiosity, she began her exploration.

On her second evening, while retracing Anne's footsteps, Sarah found herself in the deserted library, the walls lined with old tomes and lit by dim, flickering candles. She was particularly engrossed in an aged diary, believed to have been written by one of Anne's ladies-in-waiting.

As she turned the fragile pages, she stumbled upon a startling passage:

"They say her spirit roams Hever, not at peace. Some nights, when the moon is but a sliver, you can hear the soft whimper of her cries. But it's not our lovely Anne they see... it's her phantom, headless. Grief has morphed her once serene spirit into something... unholy."

A shiver cascaded down Sarah's spine. It was a tale she hadn't come across before. Engrossed, she read on, until a cold draft blew in, extinguishing the candles. The darkness felt alive, oppressive. As she fumbled for a match, she heard it—a soft, mournful whimper.

She lit a candle and its flame revealed nothing amiss. "It's just the old castle," Sarah whispered, trying to calm her racing heart.

But the whimper persisted, now joined by the eerie sound of a body moving, cloth rustling, slow footsteps drawing nearer. Sarah's breath caught in her throat as she slowly turned. And then she saw it: the shadowy silhouette of a woman in a Tudor gown, moving with an elegant grace that belied its ghostly nature. The figure moved closer, the candlelight revealing a chilling detail—the body was headless.

Sarah's scream pierced the silent library, and she stumbled backward, knocking over a stack of books. The ghostly figure floated closer, her headless body emanating an intense sorrow. Sarah scrambled to her feet, rushing out of the library, her heart pounding louder than the castle's ancient clocks.

She bolted straight into John, the castle's elderly caretaker, nearly knocking him off his feet. With panic evident in her eyes, she recounted her encounter. He listened, his face turning grave.

"Many have seen her," he whispered, "but she shows herself to only those she believes can help. I reckon she's chosen you, Miss Sarah."

Sarah looked at him, incredulous. "Help? How?"

John shared a local legend, which stated that Anne's spirit could only be freed by a heartfelt prayer, offered by a true believer in her innocence, in the very room of her apparition.

Sarah's scepticism warred with the undeniable truth of what she had witnessed. But as a historian, she felt an inexplicable duty towards the restless soul. She decided to act on the legend.

Late that night, with John standing watch outside, Sarah re-entered the library. She lit all the candles, illuminating every dark corner, and took a deep breath, recalling all she'd learned about Anne Boleyn's tragic life.

Whispers of the past swirled around her as she began to speak, her voice trembling yet firm. "Anne Boleyn, wronged queen, I believe in your innocence. Let the heavens hear this plea and grant you the peace you've long been denied."

The candles flickered wildly, and the temperature dropped sharply. Then, the headless apparition emerged, radiating a deep blue hue. But instead of the mournful wail, there was a palpable sense of peace. The spectre floated closer, stopping a few feet away from Sarah.

In a heart-stopping moment, the headless form began to transform. The severed neck mended itself, and a beautiful, yet sorrowful face appeared—Anne Boleyn in her prime. She regarded Sarah with tear-filled eyes, her lips moving in a silent 'thank you.' And then, with a final, serene glance, she faded away, the oppressive aura of the library lifting.

Sarah, overwhelmed, slumped into a chair, tears streaming down her face. She had witnessed the impossible, felt the depths of a tormented soul, and perhaps, set it free.

John, entering the library, found her shaken but intact. "It's done then?" he asked softly.

She nodded. "She's free."

But Hever Castle, ancient and filled with memories, had more tales yet to tell. As Sarah and John left the library, a mournful cry echoed through the halls. Another spirit, another story, waiting to be told and to be set free.

But Sarah knew that some stories, no matter how compelling, were best left untold. She left Hever the next day, the haunting memory of Anne Boleyn's headless apparition forever imprinted in her mind, a chilling reminder of the thin line that separated the past from the present.

CHAPTER 42:

The Spectres of Avebury Stone Circles, Wiltshire

Julie Harmon had a strange obsession with old stones. Perhaps it was a byproduct of being a geologist's daughter, or perhaps it was the one summer she had spent with her grandmother in Cornwall, listening to tales of druids and ancient rituals. When she read about the Avebury Stone Circles in Wiltshire, her fascination couldn't be contained. Older and grander than Stonehenge, Avebury promised a portal to the ancient past.

She packed her bags, camera, notebook, and a small pendulum that her grandmother had given her. "It reacts to energy fields," her grandmother had whispered, "especially the old ones."

The village of Avebury was quaint, its streets flanked with ivy-clad houses. It seemed strange to Julie that an entire village could be enclosed within an ancient stone circle. But as she drew closer to the stones, that curiosity transformed into a suffocating feeling of reverence. The stones, weathered and worn, stood like ancient sentinels against the march of time.

Julie walked among them, pendulum in hand. She felt silly, watching the small metal piece dangle lifelessly. But when she approached one of the larger stones, the pendulum began to rotate vigorously, forming tight little circles.

She jotted notes, sketched, and took pictures. The sun began its descent, casting long shadows that made the monoliths seem even more foreboding.

As twilight approached, Julie noticed that the village was strangely silent. There were no children playing, no sounds of evening meals being prepared. An eerie stillness settled over the place.

Drawn by some inexplicable force, Julie made her way to the outer circle. Here, the stones were more spaced out, standing like guardians to some ancient realm. Between two of the largest stones, she felt a sudden drop in temperature. Trusting her instincts, she let the pendulum hang freely. It swung with such force towards one of the stones that it almost wrenched itself from her grip.

Julie's heart raced. The stories of phantoms and pagan rituals, which she had brushed off as mere myths, now echoed loudly in her mind.

Suddenly, soft murmurs filled the air. They grew louder, transforming into chants that seemed both far away and all around her. The ground vibrated subtly beneath her feet, resonating with the rhythm of the chants.

From the corners of her eyes, she glimpsed figures – ethereal, translucent, almost shadow-like, dancing around the stones. They wore robes, their faces obscured by hoods, but their hands were raised, and in them, they held torches that burned with a ghostly blue flame. The figures moved in synchrony, their steps measured, their voices joining the chants that now filled the air.

Julie, paralyzed with fear, hid behind one of the stones. She dared a peek and saw that at the centre of this spectral congregation stood a raised stone platform. On it lay a figure, seemingly lifeless.

The chanting grew frenetic. One of the robed figures, taller and seemingly more substantial than the others, approached the platform, a dagger gleaming in its hand. As the dagger descended, a piercing scream rent the air.

Julie's terror reached its zenith. She ran, but her feet felt heavy, the ground beneath her turning to treacle, resisting her every step. The ghostly figures turned their attention to her, their chants now a cacophonous roar. The torches they held blazed brighter, illuminating their skeletal faces beneath the hoods.

She felt hands – cold, insubstantial, yet impossibly strong – grabbing at her, pulling her towards the platform. The dagger, still dripping with ethereal blood, was raised again, pointing directly at her heart.

Suddenly, a loud, resonant bell began to toll. The figures hissed in what sounded like pain and retreated. The spectral world around her started to dissolve, the robed figures, the platform, the ghostly torches all fading into the gathering mist.

Julie found herself standing alone among the stones, the first rays of dawn breaking the horizon. The pendulum, lying discarded on the ground, was still.

Shaken, she made her way back to the village inn. The innkeeper, a wrinkled old man with wise eyes, met her gaze. "You've seen them, haven't you?" he asked, his voice barely above a whisper.

Julie could only nod, her voice lost.

"Every year, on this very night," the innkeeper began, "they return, reenacting the rituals of old, searching for a soul to complete their circle."

"But why? Who are they?"

The innkeeper sighed. "No one knows for sure. Some say they are the spirits of the ancient druids, bound to the stones because of a ritual gone wrong. Others believe they are the guardians of the circle, ensuring that the old ways are not forgotten."

Julie shuddered. "Why didn't you warn me?"

"Few believe the tales, and those who've seen them rarely return. You are one of the lucky ones."

Julie left Avebury that morning, the images of the ghostly ritual still vivid in her mind. But as the years passed, the memories faded, becoming indistinct like a half-remembered dream.

Yet, every year, on the anniversary of that night, she would wake up to find a small stone placed beside her bed – a silent, chilling reminder of the night she had witnessed the spectres of Avebury Stone Circles.

CHAPTER 43:

The Ghosts of Athelhampton House, Dorset

Athelhampton House, with its stately Tudor architecture and breathtaking gardens, stood as a testament to time. Nestled deep in the heart of Dorset, this historic manor was a masterpiece of preserved heritage.

Emma, a 27-year-old journalist from London, was dispatched to write a piece about the history of the house. While she appreciated the chance to leave the city's hustle and bustle, her real passion was investigative journalism, exposing political scandals, or digging into corporate malfeasance. Still, a job was a job.

Upon arrival, the beauty of Athelhampton took her breath away. The gravel crunched beneath her feet as she made her way to the grand entrance. However, it wasn't just the architectural beauty that intrigued her. Rumours whispered of apparitions, the famed Grey Lady, and a pet ape that had supposedly been entombed within the walls, left behind and forgotten.

Mr. Catherwood, the current custodian of the house, greeted her. An old man, thin and wiry, with sharp eyes that seemed to pierce right through her. He guided her through the magnificent rooms, regaling her with tales from history, and occasionally hinting at the spectres that were believed to haunt the manor.

But Emma was a sceptic. "Ghosts are for children and those with overactive imaginations," she had often declared. She believed in what she could see, touch, and prove.

Night fell, and Emma was granted permission to stay overnight, allowing her to write her piece in the very ambiance of the manor. Mr. Catherwood showed her to a lavish bedroom. Before leaving, he leaned in, his voice barely a whisper, "Be wary after dark, Miss. The house has many tales, and not all of them are kind."

Left alone, Emma unpacked and started her work, tapping away at her laptop. Hours passed, and she decided to take a break, wandering the dimly lit corridors. She felt an uncanny coldness, even though it was summer. Shadows seemed to dance and move just out of her line of sight.

As she passed a grand mirror, she froze. Reflected behind her was a woman draped in grey, her face obscured by a hood. Emma spun around. No one. She glanced back at the mirror. Her own reflection stared back, solitary.

Shaken but refusing to give in to her fears, Emma continued her exploration. Upon entering the library, she felt an oppressive weight. Rows of books lined the walls, some ancient and covered in dust. In the dim light, she noticed something odd about one wall. Approaching it, she saw a slight gap in the wood panelling.

Curiosity compelled her to push against it. The panel swung open, revealing a hidden room. Inside, a skeletal form lay on the floor, the bones small and oddly shaped. A pet ape, she realized. But what truly caught her eye was the diary beside it.

Picking it up, Emma began to read. The diary belonged to Lady Elizabeth, the rumoured 'Grey Lady.' The entries described her loneliness and her only solace: her pet ape. As she turned the pages, the entries became darker, hinting at a forbidden relationship between Elizabeth and a servant. The last entry was unsettling. It spoke of a plan to escape with her lover and the ape, to start anew. But the diary ended abruptly.

Suddenly, the temperature dropped. Emma felt a presence, the weight of sorrow thick in the air. She heard soft sobbing. Turning around, the Grey Lady stood before her, her figure clearer now. Beside her, the spectral form of an ape.

Emma felt a mix of terror and sympathy. Elizabeth reached out, her hand cold as death, touching Emma's face. Flashes of memories not her own flooded Emma's mind. Scenes of love, betrayal, and a tragic end. The servant, her lover, had been paid off by Elizabeth's family, leaving Elizabeth alone and heartbroken. In her despair, she had locked herself and her pet ape in the hidden room, where both met their tragic demise.

Emma collapsed, overwhelmed by the sheer intensity of the emotions. When she awoke, daylight streamed into the library. The hidden room was still open, but the diary and the skeletal remains were gone. It was as if they had never existed.

Hurrying to her room, she packed her things, eager to leave. She felt a newfound respect for the spirits that roamed the manor, especially Elizabeth and her tragic story.

Mr. Catherwood saw her out, his sharp eyes assessing her. "You've seen her, haven't you?"

Emma nodded, her voice barely audible. "I have, and I understand her pain."

As she drove away, she glanced back. At the window of the room she had stayed in, the figure of the Grey Lady stood, watching her, the spectral ape by her side. The last thing Emma heard as she sped away was the soft, mournful sobbing carried by the wind.

Haunted by her experience, Emma wrote an evocative piece about Athelhampton House, blending history with the supernatural. It became her most celebrated work. However, she never returned to the manor, the memories too raw and powerful.

And so, Athelhampton House stands, its beauty masking the sorrow and tragedy within its walls, waiting for the next visitor to unveil its secrets.

CHAPTER 44:

The Spirit of Margaret Pomeroy, Berry Pomeroy Castle, Devon

The rain splattered across the windscreen as Harry Benson's wipers worked overtime. He had travelled south to Devon to delve into the rich tapestry of British history for his thesis on haunted castles. Berry Pomeroy was one on his list. Known not just for its breathtaking ruins, but also for the tragic tale of Margaret Pomeroy.

The legend whispered of two sisters - Margaret and Eleanor - and a jealousy so profound that it turned to wickedness. Eleanor, maddened by jealousy, imprisoned Margaret in the dungeons below the castle, leaving her to starve to death.

Arriving at the visitor's centre, Harry paid for his entry and took a map. The lady at the counter, a lady with a sharp, angular face and pale eyes, looked him dead in the eye and said, "Mind the dungeons, lad."

"Legends don't scare me," Harry replied, with a cocky grin.

She just muttered, "You'll see."

The castle's ruins stood against the grey backdrop of the sky, creating an ominous feel. Harry started his exploration from the main hall and slowly made his way towards the dungeons. He'd brought a torch with him, as he'd been told the lower parts of the castle were shrouded in perpetual darkness.

Navigating his way through, he felt a sudden drop in temperature. The stories had said that this was where Eleanor imprisoned her sister. The torch flickered as Harry felt a cold breeze. He paused, listening. From the dark recesses of the dungeon, he heard a soft, haunting melody. A woman's voice, singing a melancholic lullaby.

Curiosity piqued, he moved towards the sound. The stone walls seemed to close in, the singing grew louder. His torch fell upon a sight that made his heart race. A figure of a woman, with long, flowing hair, sat chained to the wall, her translucent form glowing slightly.

She looked up, her eyes hollow from despair. "Help me," she whispered.

Harry's mind raced. This couldn't be real. It was just a legend.

But then, another form emerged. A darker figure. Eleanor.

"You shouldn't have come here," she hissed.

Margaret's ghostly form floated towards Harry, "Save me."

Eleanor lunged, but her form passed through Harry, leaving him with a feeling of absolute cold. Margaret's chains rattled loudly as her form became more and more corporeal. The air grew heavier.

Harry's logic and reason battled with what he was witnessing. "How can I help you?" he managed to say.

"Find my remains, give me a proper burial," Margaret's voice was a whisper but carried a weight of centuries of pain.

A sinister laughter echoed. Eleanor's spirit swirled around them, "You can't help her. She's mine forever."

Margaret's apparition pointed towards a corner. Harry's torch illuminated an old wooden box, almost decayed with time. Inside were skeletal remains, a small pendant with the initial 'M' lay beside them.

Eleanor's angry howls filled the chamber. "You cannot break the curse!"

Gathering his courage, Harry took the pendant and the remains. Margaret's form glowed brighter, and she pointed him towards the exit. But Eleanor wasn't going to let them go so easily. The dungeon started to shake, stones fell from above, and a dark mist enveloped them.

Battling his fear and the obstacles Eleanor threw in his path, Harry managed to make it out of the dungeons. The storm outside had intensified. The rain was torrential.

With Margaret guiding him, he reached the castle's old burial grounds. He dug a makeshift grave, placed the remains inside, and covered them. As he did, the storm began to wane.

The pendant in his hand glowed. Margaret's form appeared, but she looked different, at peace. "Thank you," she whispered and slowly faded away.

But as Harry turned to leave, Eleanor's enraged spirit descended upon him. "You may have saved her, but you cannot save yourself!" The surroundings became a whirlwind of darkness. Eleanor's laughter echoed as Harry felt himself being dragged back towards the dungeons.

The next morning, the lady from the visitor's centre found a notebook near the castle ruins. Flipping through the pages, she found detailed notes on various castles and the story of Margaret Pomeroy.

As she walked back to the centre, she muttered, "I did warn him."

Every year, there would be someone, driven by curiosity, wanting to explore the haunted dungeons of Berry Pomeroy. Some left unscathed, but others, like Harry, were never seen again. For the spirits that reside there, especially Eleanor, were never truly at rest. And their malevolence knew no bounds.

CHAPTER 45:

The Screaming Woods of Dering, Kent

Darkness had a unique presence in the woods of Dering. The oaks and elms were old, their limbs stretching towards the heavens as if begging for salvation from the secrets they held within their knotted bark. On clear nights, the stars twinkled through gaps in the canopy, casting a silvery light onto the forest floor. Yet, on this particular night, the clouds hung low and heavy, leaving the woods to be swallowed by an impenetrable black.

Rory hadn't meant to find himself there at night. He'd started his walk early, hoping to enjoy a pleasant day exploring the woods he'd heard so much about. Legends spoke of lost souls that wandered the woods, forever severed from the world of the living. He had always been a sceptic, dismissing ghost stories as mere folklore. But as darkness fell and he realized he had lost his way, a sense of unease began to take hold.

The woods were silent, save for the soft rustle of fallen leaves beneath his feet. The very air seemed stagnant, as if time had stopped and trapped him within its void. Rory tried calling out, but his voice felt smothered by the trees.

A chilling breeze cut through the woods. Trees whispered to each other in soft, conspiratorial tones. Rory felt his hair stand on end. And then he heard it.

A scream. A blood-curdling, heart-wrenching scream. It echoed around him, coming from every direction at once. It sounded neither male nor female, neither young nor old. It was a raw, guttural cry of pure agony and despair.

He began to run, desperate to escape the source of the scream. But as he ran, more voices joined the chorus. They wailed and sobbed, their cries piercing through the thick canopy. Panic consumed him. He could feel eyes on him, watching his every move.

Suddenly, he stumbled upon a clearing. The grass was a luminous shade of green, almost glowing in the surrounding darkness. In the middle stood an old stone well, its sides worn and covered in moss.

Drawn to it, Rory approached cautiously. The cries seemed softer here, almost muted. He peered over the edge, half-expecting to see something unspeakable. But the well was empty, its bottom filled with dried leaves and twigs.

Rory felt a strange compulsion to climb inside, as if the well promised shelter from the relentless voices that filled the woods. He swung his legs over the edge and began his descent, his feet searching for crevices and cracks in the stone.

Halfway down, he paused. The screams had stopped. It was eerily silent. The only sound was his own breath echoing off the stone walls. He felt trapped, ensnared by the very sanctuary he had sought.

Then, a soft whisper reached his ears. "Join us."

Rory looked up. Standing around the well were shadowy figures, their eyes hollow and faces expressionless. Men, women, children, all staring down at him, their voices joining in a haunting melody.

He felt an unseen force pulling him down, trying to drag him into the depths of the well. He fought against it, clutching onto the sides of the well, his fingers scraping against the stone.

The figures began to wail, their cries echoing down the well, consuming him. He could feel their pain, their suffering. It wrapped around him, pulling him deeper and deeper.

Rory screamed, his voice joining the chorus of the lost souls. His grip loosened, and he felt himself being pulled into the abyss. The last thing he heard before everything went black was the mournful cries of the spirits, forever trapped in the Screaming Woods of Dering.

Years passed, and the legend of the Screaming Woods grew. Locals warned visitors to stay away, especially at night. But every so often, a brave soul would venture into the woods, only to be claimed by its malevolent spirits.

On a particularly dark night, a group of thrill-seekers, having heard the tales, decided to test their courage. As they stepped into the woods, they felt the weight of countless eyes upon them. The air grew cold, and an oppressive silence enveloped them.

Then, from the distance, a scream echoed, followed by more, creating a symphony of terror. The group clutched onto each other, paralyzed with fear. They heard whispers, soft and seductive, drawing them deeper into the woods. "Join us."

In the centre of a luminous clearing stood an old stone well. Curiosity drew them closer, and as they peered inside, they saw a figure, his eyes hollow, his face expressionless.

Rory, now one of the many spirits trapped in the Screaming Woods, whispered, his voice filled with eternal despair, "Join us."

CHAPTER 46:

The Highgate Vampire, Highgate Cemetery, London

In the early 1970s, Highgate Cemetery wasn't the neatly manicured and carefully tended burial ground it had once been. Graves lay obscured under wild overgrowth, paths faded into dark thickets, and the air carried the decay of time. But it wasn't just the tombstones that were hidden away; something far more sinister lurked in the shadows.

David Crowley, a historian and amateur paranormal investigator, lived nearby. Every morning, as part of his daily ritual, David would take a brisk walk through the cemetery. He was researching a book on Victorian death rituals, and the cemetery was his muse. Each day, he made sketches, jotted down inscriptions from the gravestones, and allowed the stories of those long passed to seep into his mind.

One particularly chilly morning in December, as mist rolled across the path, David noticed a group of people gathered around one of the larger mausoleums. Their eyes, though hidden under the brims of hats and hoods, were wide with fear. He approached cautiously.

"What's going on?" David asked.

A woman, trembling, pointed towards the mausoleum's door. "There's something... inside."

He took a step closer, listening intently. A faint, irregular scratching emanated from the stone structure. He felt a chill crawl up his spine – it wasn't the cold of winter.

The group, made up of locals, began to whisper among themselves about a vampire that had recently taken residence in Highgate. The tales varied. Some spoke of a tall, dark figure with burning red eyes, while others talked about a ghostly spectre that exuded an icy cold aura.

Intrigued and somewhat sceptical, David decided to investigate further. He began by interviewing those who claimed to have had encounters with the creature. The testimonies were harrowing: dreams of being pursued through the cemetery, sensations of cold breath on one's neck, and even unexplainable marks on their bodies.

One testimony stood out. A young woman named Alice spoke of a horrifying dream in which she was chased by a dark figure with piercing red eyes. When she awoke, she found herself outside her home, standing at the cemetery's entrance, with no memory of how she got there.

As winter deepened, more and more residents reported similar encounters. The cemetery became a hub for vampire hunters and thrill-seekers, each hoping to catch a glimpse of the Highgate Vampire.

David wasn't one to believe in vampires, but he couldn't ignore the mounting evidence. He decided to conduct a vigil, setting up cameras and audio equipment around the most frequently reported spots.

The first few nights were uneventful, but on the fourth night, as the moon hid behind dark clouds, David heard a sound that made his heart race: a soft, haunting whisper, so faint that he wasn't sure if he'd imagined it. Following the sound, he came upon a freshly dug grave. The earth around it looked disturbed, and the scent of decay was strong.

Drawing closer, he felt a sudden drop in temperature. Then, from the darkness of a nearby tree, a tall, shadowy figure emerged. It was dressed in tattered Victorian clothing, its face obscured by the darkness, save for two glowing red eyes that stared directly at him.

David's breath caught in his throat, and his first instinct was to run. But his legs felt rooted to the spot. As the figure approached, David felt a coldness envelop him, not just of temperature, but a deep, soul-chilling cold that seemed to drain the very life out of him.

The entity moved closer, and David could now see its face – pale, gaunt, with sharp, elongated fangs protruding from its mouth. It reached out a withered hand, fingers ending in sharp talons.

As the creature's fingers brushed against his skin, David felt an overwhelming despair. Images flooded his mind: all the people buried in the cemetery, their last moments, their regrets, and their unfulfilled dreams.

With a final surge of strength, he managed to break free, stumbling back and colliding with a tombstone. The creature, seemingly displeased, retreated into the shadows.

Gasping for breath, David grabbed his equipment and fled. He didn't stop until he reached the safety of his home. Locking all doors and windows, he collapsed onto his couch, heart pounding.

Over the next few days, David tried to make sense of what he'd experienced. He researched deeper into the cemetery's history and discovered an old legend about a nobleman from Eastern Europe who'd been buried in Highgate in the late 1800s. Rumoured to have dabbled in the dark arts, it was said that he could never truly die.

David knew he couldn't let the creature continue its reign of terror. Gathering a group of locals, they ventured to the mausoleum where the nobleman was said to be interred. Inside, in the pitch black, they found a coffin. Opening it revealed not a decaying corpse but a perfectly preserved body.

As they stood there, the temperature dropped, and the familiar shadowy figure emerged. The group, armed with stakes and holy water, advanced. The creature hissed, its red eyes flaring with rage.

A fierce battle ensued. David, drawing from a deep reservoir of courage, managed to drive a stake through the creature's heart. It let out an ear-piercing scream before disintegrating into dust.

The group left the mausoleum, sealing it shut. The terror that had gripped Highgate seemed to be over. However, David's ordeal was far from finished. Every night, he was plagued by nightmares of the creature, its glowing eyes, and the cold touch of its hand.

The locals spoke of how the Highgate Vampire had been defeated, but for David, it was a constant presence. One night, as he lay in bed, paralyzed by another nightmare, he felt a familiar coldness envelop him. Opening his eyes, he found himself not in his room but in the cemetery.

Before him stood the creature, its red eyes glowing even more intensely. It spoke in a haunting whisper, "You may have defeated my physical form, but I will always be here, in your mind, in your nightmares."

David tried to scream, but no sound came out. The creature's laugh echoed through the cold night, and darkness consumed everything.

The next morning, locals found David's lifeless body at the entrance of Highgate Cemetery. The terror of the Highgate Vampire might have been quelled, but its curse lived on, a chilling reminder that some evils can never truly be vanquished.

CHAPTER 47:

The Green Children of Woolpit

The rain was relentless in Woolpit, Suffolk. It began as a light drizzle, then intensified into a heavy downpour. Most days, the village streets would be filled with children playing, old men recounting tales at the local pub, and ladies going about their errands. But on this particular day, an eerie silence enveloped Woolpit, pierced only by the pitter-patter of the rain.

Martha, a middle-aged woman known for her charitable work and her impeccable apple pies, peered through the window of her thatched-roof cottage. The mist was thickening, rendering visibility nearly nil. She sighed, shaking her head, "What an odd day."

She was about to turn away when movement caught her eye. Two small figures, emerging from the woods, were staggering towards the village, their movements erratic and unsteady. Children. One older, possibly around twelve, and a younger one, maybe eight. Their clothes, if they could be called that, were ragged, hanging off their bony frames. But it was their skin that made Martha gasp in disbelief: it was green, an unnatural shade, like moss-covered stones.

Unsure of what she was seeing, Martha dashed out of her house, her feet splashing in the muddy water. The two children were now in the town square, drawing attention.

People emerged from their homes, whispers of shock and disbelief weaving through the rain-soaked air. The children seemed disoriented, their wide eyes filled with terror.

"Who are they? Where did they come from?" The murmurs grew louder.

Martha, driven by a maternal instinct, approached them slowly, her voice soft. "It's alright. You're safe here." She opened her arms to offer warmth, and the older child hesitated only for a second before collapsing into her embrace, the younger one following suit.

Over the next few days, the village was abuzz with speculation. Theories ran wild, ranging from them being forest spirits, to alien beings, to victims of some cruel experiment. No one had any concrete answers. The children refused to—or were unable to—speak in a recognizable language. Instead, they communicated in a series of haunting hums and melancholic melodies.

They wouldn't eat anything provided, turning away plates of hearty meals and bowls of warm soup. But when beans, fresh from the garden, were presented, they ate them raw with a fervour, their green fingers trembling.

Martha took them in, and nights were the hardest. The children sang eerie lullabies that sent shivers down one's spine. Their green eyes, which looked black in the dim candlelight, would fixate on something unseen in the corners of the room, and they would hum a tune so sombre it made Martha's heart ache.

One evening, as the village was settling into its nocturnal silence, a stranger arrived. Dressed in a cloak that covered him from head to toe, only his eyes—intense and piercing—were visible. He went straight to the local inn, demanding to see the green children.

Edward, the innkeeper, had heard the tales but hadn't seen the children himself. He was intrigued, but wary. "Who are you? Why do you seek them?"

The stranger's voice was like gravel, rough and chilling. "I know where they come from. I've been searching for them."

Word travelled fast in small villages. By the time the stranger reached Martha's cottage, half the village had gathered, forming a protective barrier.

The older child, seeing the cloaked figure, started to hum a tune—different from before, frenzied and anxious. The younger one clung to Martha, trembling.

The stranger spoke, his voice echoing with a dark authority. "They don't belong here. They belong with me."

The village priest, Father Williams, stepped forward, holding his cross. "If you mean to harm them, you'll have to go through us."

A laugh, devoid of humour, erupted from the stranger. With a swift movement, he lowered his hood, revealing green-tinted skin, much darker than the children's. His eyes were voids of blackness.

"They're not what you think," he hissed. "They're harbingers. Wherever they go, misfortune follows. Your crops will fail, your livestock will perish, and your children... they will be next."

The crowd gasped. Some whispered prayers, others held onto their loved ones. The night, filled with tension, seemed to close in on them.

"Return them, and I may spare your village."

Martha, her voice shaking but defiant, stepped forward. "They're scared of you. I won't let you take them."

The stranger's voice grew cold. "Then suffer the consequences."

Suddenly, the ground trembled, the skies roared, and an overwhelming darkness consumed the village. When the light returned, the stranger and the green children were gone.

Days turned into weeks. The stranger's words proved true. The once-prosperous village was now a shadow of its former self. Despair was in the air, punctuated by frequent cries of mourning.

Martha, filled with guilt, would often be seen at the edge of the woods, humming the tunes the green children once sang, hoping, praying, they'd return.

But they never did.

And as the years passed, the village of Woolpit faded from maps, its existence erased. All that remained were whispers of green children and the haunting lullabies that echoed in the wind.

CHAPTER 48:

The Gwyllgi, the Dog of Darkness in Wales

The sun had long vanished beyond the horizon, allowing the dark, thick cloak of night to swallow the tiny Welsh village of Llandwyr. Under the dim light of the moon, which peeked intermittently between clouds, the hallowed streets echoed with the eerie whistle of wind. Occasionally, a wild rabbit or two might dart across a garden, but the town slept – or at least, it seemed to.

Evan was the exception.

He was an avid jogger. Llandwyr was not the sort of place most would choose for a midnight run, but Evan was not most people. He thrived on the challenge, on the unpredictability of the uneven terrains, on the dark. More importantly, he relished the silence, with only his panting breaths and rhythmic footfalls for company. Tonight was no different. Or so he thought.

As Evan began his routine, he noticed something odd: a mist swirling along the pathway ahead. It wasn't the sort of fog you'd associate with a chilly night, but more like black smoke, rising and spreading outwards.

He slowed down, his eyes squinting in an attempt to discern the source of this strange phenomenon. And then, a faint sound reached his ears – a low growl, one that seemed to resonate with the most primitive and ancient of fears.

Evan froze. Out from the mist emerged a large, spectral black dog. Its eyes glowed a piercing crimson, and a low rumble emitted from its throat, echoing the unsettling growl he'd heard earlier. The air grew cold, and a thick, oppressing tension weighed down upon Evan. He was in the presence of the Gwyllgi, the mythical Dog of Darkness that haunted the Welsh roads.

Panicking, Evan turned to retreat, but his legs refused to move. He was paralyzed, rooted to the spot, caught in the infernal gaze of the beast. Every local legend he'd ever heard about the creature played in his mind. How it would often appear on lonely roads, its stare alone capable of inflicting unspeakable terror on its victim.

Its legend wasn't without tragedy. Decades ago, a miner named Ianto was said to have encountered the Gwyllgi on his way home. The next morning, his lifeless body was found on the road, his face contorted in a perpetual scream, his eyes wide open in terror.

Evan's heartbeat drummed loudly in his ears, but the Gwyllgi merely watched him, its fiery eyes scanning him, almost reading his very soul. The seconds felt like hours.

Just as Evan thought his heart would burst from sheer terror, a distant sound snapped him from the spell – a church bell, tolling midnight. The beast's head jerked up, and with a swift motion, it vanished into the mist, leaving Evan gasping for breath.

The next morning, Evan related his ordeal to his grandmother, a stoic woman with deep knowledge of local legends. She listened intently, her weathered face showing no emotion until he finished.

"You've been marked," she whispered gravely.

Evan blinked. "Marked?"

"The Gwyllgi doesn't appear for no reason. It's either an omen or a curse. You need to make peace, child, with whatever darkness you've been hiding," she said, her gaze unflinching.

Evan's mind raced. He had no secrets, no darkness. Or did he? There was that incident years ago, a hit-and-run. He'd been drunk, and in a panic, fled the scene, leaving behind an injured dog. He never spoke of it, burying the guilt deep within.

Could this be the source of the haunting?

Feeling a desperate need to right his wrongs, Evan visited the spot of the accident. The rusty remains of an old gate marked the place. As memories flooded back, Evan knelt, tears streaming down his face. "I'm sorry," he whispered to the night.

The wind howled in response, and once again, the Gwyllgi emerged from the shadows, but this time, it wasn't alone. Beside it stood another, much smaller figure – the very dog Evan had hit all those years ago.

Both animals approached him. The smaller dog's wounds still fresh, it limped over and nuzzled Evan's hand, a forgiving gesture that tugged at his heartstrings.

But the Gwyllgi was not here for forgiveness. It circled Evan, growling softly. The understanding was clear: the smaller dog might have forgiven Evan, but the Gwyllgi, the embodiment of darkness and retribution, had other plans.

It lunged. Evan's screams pierced the cold night, echoing through the woods, a chilling reminder of the consequences of past sins.

By morning, the villagers found him. Just like Ianto, Evan lay lifeless, his face frozen in horror. And though the Dog of Darkness had claimed another soul, the tragic tale of Evan served as a chilling reminder to all: in the face of ancient legends, one's past always comes back to haunt.

The legend of the Gwyllgi lived on, whispered from one generation to the next, a tale of horror, of darkness, of retribution, and of a debt that was always collected.

CHAPTER 49:

The Black Lady of Bradley Woods, Lincolnshire

The streets of Lincolnshire were quiet. The kind of quiet that unsettled one's soul, sending tingling sensations down the spine. The village seemed almost abandoned, save for the chirping of a distant cricket and the rustling of unseen creatures in the underbrush.

The moonlight was broken by dark clouds, and everything was bathed in its pale glow. But there was one part of Lincolnshire that locals rarely visited, especially after sunset: Bradley Woods.

An old sign, nearly obliterated by decades of weather and neglect, cautioned: Bradley Woods – Tread at Your Own Risk.

Dave had heard about the woods during his brief stint at the local pub. "Stay away from there after dark," the old barkeep had warned him, a nervous glance given to the clock hanging above the doorway. But Dave, a newcomer to the village and a sceptic of all things supernatural, had shrugged off the old man's warning.

Dave, with his lanky frame, prominent Adam's apple, and a mop of curly brown hair, considered himself a modern man. A man of science and reason. To him, ghosts and goblins were stories to tell children around a campfire. He was more intrigued than afraid.

He had moved to Lincolnshire just a month ago for a research job. And tonight, armed with a flashlight and his insatiable curiosity, he decided to take a walk into the infamous Bradley Woods.

As he ventured deeper, he felt an unnatural chill envelop him, seeping through his light jacket and making his hairs stand on end. But it was not the temperature that unsettled Dave. It was the silence.

He realized that the normal cacophony of the woods, the rustling leaves, and chirping crickets were conspicuously absent. Instead, there was an almost tangible feeling of expectancy, as if the woods themselves were holding their breath.

It was then that he saw her.

Standing a short distance away, just beyond the reach of his flashlight's beam, was a woman draped in a black hooded cloak. Her face was hidden in the shadows, but he could make out her tear-filled eyes that sparkled with the reflected moonlight.

Dave froze, his heart hammering in his chest. Every logical bone in his body told him to turn back, to run, but curiosity kept his feet rooted to the spot.

"Who are you?" he managed to choke out.

Her voice was a whisper, a soft lament carried by the wind. "Have you seen my child?"

Dave blinked. "Your child?"

"My baby," she sobbed. "I've been searching for him for centuries. Have you seen him?"

Dave's scepticism began to waver. He had heard legends of the Black Lady, a grieving mother from medieval times searching for her lost child. But he never thought he'd meet her face to face.

"No, I haven't," he replied. His voice was quivering despite his best efforts to keep it steady.

Suddenly, a gust of wind rushed through the trees, and the Black Lady seemed to dissolve into the shadows, her mournful wail echoing through the woods.

As he stood there, shock beginning to set in, he heard a soft whimpering sound from behind him. Turning slowly, he saw a small, shadowy figure of a child, his face obscured, standing a few feet away. The child pointed deeper into the woods, beckoning Dave to follow.

Against his better judgment, Dave found himself being drawn towards the child. The deeper they went, the more oppressive the atmosphere became. The trees seemed to close in on him, and he could feel unseen eyes watching his every move.

After what felt like hours, they reached a clearing. In the centre stood an ancient, gnarled tree, its branches twisting and turning like tortured souls. Hanging from one of the branches was a small, tattered baby's blanket, swaying gently in the breeze.

The child pointed towards it, tears streaming down his face.

"That's mine," he whispered. "She left me here."

Dave felt a chill run down his spine. "Who left you?"

The child pointed again, this time towards the edge of the clearing. The Black Lady stood there, her eyes filled with an unimaginable sadness. "I was so scared," she whispered. "The world was a cruel place. I thought he'd be safe here."

Dave felt a pang of pity for the tortured soul. "You can be together now," he said, trying to sound reassuring.

But as he spoke, the atmosphere shifted. The sorrow was replaced by an overwhelming sense of anger and malevolence.

"You!" the Black Lady hissed, her face contorting into a mask of rage. "You brought him here! You separated us!"

Dave backed away, his heart racing. "No! I didn't! I just found him!"

But it was too late. The Black Lady lunged at him, her fingers outstretched, her eyes glowing with an unearthly light.

Dave tried to scream, but no sound came out. His flashlight flickered and died, plunging the woods into darkness.

When morning came, the locals found Dave's lifeless body at the edge of Bradley Woods, his face contorted in terror. The flashlight lay next to him, its beam still weakly shining towards the ancient tree.

The Black Lady and her child had vanished, but the legend lived on. And Dave became another chapter in the eerie tales of Bradley Woods, a warning to all who dared to venture into the realm of the unknown.

CHAPTER 50:

The Blue Lady of Temple Newsam, Leeds

In the vastness of Yorkshire, the Temple Newsam estate stood as a testament to opulence and history. An architectural marvel, the house boasted Tudor-Jacobean features that rendered it a spectacle for many. It was not just its grandiose facade that made it famous, but rather the legends and tales of those who once lived within its walls.

The Ingram family was among its most notable residents. It was said that centuries ago, a tragic event befell Mary Ingram, the youngest and most vivacious of the family, which led to her untimely demise. Now, as the story goes, she wanders the halls, restlessly searching for her lost pearls, forever draped in a flowing blue gown, earning her the name - The Blue Lady.

Jason, an urban explorer and paranormal enthusiast, had heard of Mary's tale. His insatiable curiosity had taken him to many haunted spots, but Temple Newsam was the one he was most anxious about. He had been warned of its malevolent energy, how those who dared disturb Mary's spirit suffered dire consequences. Yet, driven by an obsession to document the otherworldly, Jason decided to spend a night at the manor.

The sun had barely set when Jason started his exploration. Armed with his camera and a torch, he began to wander the long corridors and vast rooms. The house, in its stillness, exuded an aura of dormant energy, waiting to be awakened. It was silent, but not in a peaceful way; it was the kind of silence that felt heavy, laden with unspoken tales and buried secrets.

As he wandered, he stumbled upon a portrait of Mary Ingram. A young woman, with porcelain skin and eyes that radiated a certain melancholy, stared back at him. Her blue dress, with pearls adorning the neckline, seemed almost too vivid against the dim lighting. The more Jason looked, the more he felt drawn to her. There was a story there, one he desperately wanted to unveil.

It was then that he heard it - the soft, sorrowful hum of a melody. It seemed to come from the ballroom. Intrigued, Jason followed the sound. The large wooden doors to the ballroom opened with a reluctant groan, revealing a scene from the past. Gossamer-clad dancers floated across the floor, accompanied by a haunting orchestral number. But what caught Jason's attention was the figure in blue, dancing alone, her movements elegant yet filled with despair.

Overcome with fascination, Jason approached Mary, but before he could reach her, the entire scene dissolved, leaving him in an empty, dark room. It was then that he felt a cold touch on his shoulder, making him whirl around. There stood Mary, her eyes now void of their earlier sadness, replaced by a rage that sent shivers down Jason's spine. She whispered, "You shouldn't be here."

Ignoring the primal fear that surged within him, Jason stammered, "I... I just wanted to know your story."

She moved closer, the air growing colder with each step. "You wish to know of my pain? Of the betrayal that binds me to this realm?" Her voice was an echo of anguish, and Jason felt a lump form in his throat. The gravity of his intrusion dawned upon him.

In a spectral illumination, the room transformed once more. Jason found himself in a different time, witnessing a young Mary being gifted a string of pearls by a young suitor. The joy in her eyes was palpable. But as the scene played out, he watched in horror as another figure, envious of Mary's happiness, replaced the pearls with an identical string, save for one detail - these pearls were cursed.

The vision shifted to a frantic Mary, clawing at her throat as the pearls tightened around her neck, choking the life out of her. Her once lively eyes now mirrored the fear and betrayal she felt in her final moments. The scene dissolved, and Jason was back in the ballroom, Mary's ghostly figure inches from his face.

"I search for my pearls," she hissed, "but they remain elusive. And until they're found, I remain bound. Now, you too are a part of my torment."

Suddenly, Jason felt a tightening around his neck. Gasping for breath, he clutched at the phantom pearls that threatened to strangle him. His vision blurred as Mary's lament filled the room, her sorrow echoing endlessly.

By morning, when the caretakers arrived, they found Jason's lifeless body on the ballroom floor, with a faint blue hue on his face. The tales of the Blue Lady grew darker after that night, as whispers spread about her new victim.

Those who now visit Temple Newsam, if they listen closely, can sometimes hear the sorrowful duet of Mary and Jason, forever bound in their shared tragedy, forever searching for those cursed pearls.

Beyond the Pages: Your Part in the Story

Beyond the Pages: Your Part in the Story

As the weight of history and haunting tales linger in your mind, having traversed through Britain's spectral tapestry, you, dear reader, have reached an ethereal crossroads. The tales have been told, the apparitions have shared their stories, and the chill of the unknown has, perhaps, settled deep within your bones. But now, we beckon you to step beyond the veiled curtain of the written word, to take an active role in the ongoing journey of "Haunted Britain."

The Power of Your Voice

Just as every spirit has a story, every reader possesses a unique perspective. Your experience with this book is invaluable. You've encountered the ghosts of the past, felt the eerie whispers, and perhaps even glanced over your shoulder once or twice, fearing a fleeting shadow. But your journey doesn't have to end on the last page.

By sharing your thoughts, emotions, and reflections, you can breathe life into these tales beyond the confines of the book. **Your voice has the power** to propel these stories further, ensuring that they continue to haunt, captivate, and intrigue.

Why Amazon Reviews Matter

Amazon, a platform that has connected countless readers with books, relies heavily on the feedback and insights of its vast reading community. Reviews not only provide authors and publishers with valuable insights but they also play a pivotal role in helping other readers discover new horizons.

When you pen down a review:

- **You Guide Future Readers**: Your insights can act as a beacon, guiding potential readers through the fog of countless book choices.

- **You Support Our Endeavor**: Positive feedback boosts the book's visibility, allowing us to reach a broader audience and share the chilling tales of Britain's ghostly inhabitants.

- **You Help Shape Our Journey**: Constructive feedback helps us refine our work, ensuring that future tales are even more spine-tingling.

How to Leave a Review

1. **Log into Your Amazon Account**: Head over to Amazon's website.

2. **Navigate to "Haunted Britain: 50 Ghost Stories Based on True Paranormal Encounters Across England, Scotland, and Wales"**: Use the search bar to find our book or access it from your purchase history.

3. **Click on 'Write a Customer Review'**: Share your thoughts, rate the book, and let the world know of your journey through Britain's haunted realms.

4. **Submit**: Once you're satisfied with your review, hit the submit button.

In the end, every story thrives on being told, being heard, and being shared. While the spirits of "Haunted Britain" may be tethered to the past, your voice can ensure their tales resonate in the present and echo into the future. So, dear reader, as you close this book and perhaps leave a light on tonight, remember: **Your part in the story has just begun.**